# Plastic, Copper and the Hundred Thousand Percent Markup

## How monopoly pricing has threatened contraceptive security and corrupted American medicine

Michela Dai Zovi

# TOC

**Author's note:**
When this book was first published in 2014 the price of a
ParaGard® intrauterine device was $754. By January of 2015
the price had increased to $932. The text of this book has been
modified to reflect this change.

# INTRODUCTION:
## A VERY STUPID QUESTION

T his is not a book about contraceptives. This is a book about the importance of asking thorough questions in order to get complete answers. This is a book about the power that follows from leading the line of questioning. More specifically, this book is about money.

In essence, this book addresses the following question:

Why does a medical product—a tiny piece of plastic and copper that costs twenty five cents to produce—cost under $5 in Latin America, under $20 in Europe, and nearly $1,000 in the United States?

The answer, it turns out, after the one wades through the national policy and economic theory jargon, is:

Because it can.

Within the developed world there is a general perception that, at least in the case of medicine, consumers should be protected from the same capriciousness of markets that is otherwise beneficial in the case of nonessential items—electronic gadgets and designer clothing, for example. A 2008 Organization for Economic Cooperation and Development (OECD) health policy study noted that, "The perceived potential for manufacturers to exploit a monopoly position when facing relatively inelastic demand for medicines has led many countries to regulate prices for at least some portion of the pharmaceutical market."[1] That is to say, most countries within the OECD operate with the assumption that the government should negotiate medicinal prices on behalf of their citizens, because sick people are not in a position to bargain, nor to shop around for price comparisons.

Specific mechanisms of pharmaceutical pricing will be explained in a later chapter, but for now suffice it to say that evidence indicates that The United States does not operate under the same set of assumptions. The US is unique among developed nations in that there are no limitations on how much medicines can cost, scant few limitations on by how much or how often prices can go up, and actually goes as far as to legally forbid the federal government from negotiating with pharmaceutical companies for lower prices, as well as forbid citizens from purchasing cheaper medicines from outside the country. In this respect the US approach to pharmaceuticals is in effect the worst possible amalgam of free market dogma—in which government intervention is anathema and faith is placed in market forces to find a optimal balance between supply and demand—and highly regulated environment in which suppliers are limited, frequently to the point of a state-enforced monopoly, and consumer choices are restricted to: accept an un-negotiated price from a monopolistic supplier, go without medications, break the law to import them, or physically leave the country to access them elsewhere.

This is not to be confused as an ideological anti-business diatribe. Any facile comparison between the living standards of citizens in traditionally capitalistic countries with those in historically communistic countries can demonstrate that an individual's self-interested pursuit of profit can in fact be harnessed to provide optimal outcomes for society as a whole. Overall, capitalism is good, markets are good. But there are many circumstances in which markets —especially those which are unregulated or poorly regulated—fail to bring about socially optimal outcomes, and medicinal pricing is certainly one of them. In order for markets to bring about optimal outcomes, many factors must be present, including but not limited to: easy access to information, a high level of competition, and limited social repercussions in the case of market failure. That is to say, people need to know a lot about what they are buying, have many choices of sources to buy it from, and it should matter little to other people what someone else chooses or declines to buy. The American medical industry is the complete opposite of this scenario in that prices are often proprietary and hidden from the consumer, research concerning the drugs and their safety often goes unpublished and thereby made unavailable to the consumer, drug suppliers are limited—often to the point of a monopoly— and public tax funds are affected when individuals are unable to pay for their own care. Medicine is possibly the commodity that is most in need of adequate intervention, yet, in the United States —and just about only in the United States—a solution continues to elude us.

The persistence of monopoly pricing of pharmaceuticals in the United States, despite the poor job monopoly-priced medicine does of serving American consumers' interests, is so inexplicable that it implies the possibility of "regulatory capture," which is a term Nobel laureate economist George Stigler used to describe circumstances in which a regulatory agency that was created in the public interest becomes corrupted to advance special—i.e. financial—interests. Eventually the regulatory agency comes to be dominated by the very industries it was initially designed to control, in effect corralling and capturing the consumer base to serve their ends rather than the other way around.

The intrauterine device (IUD) cannot on its own provide sufficient evidence of pharmaceutical market failure, or that the United States institutions have been corrupted by regulatory capture. But it can be used as a case study, in essence a device through which the mechanisms of US institutions can be better understood by people who might be largely unfamiliar with them.

This book originated from a passive curiosity. Why are IUDs so expensive? There is a multitude of research articles concluding that the IUD is the most cost-effective contraceptive option in the American pharmacopeia, but not a single one that addresses why it should cost several times as much in the US as it does in Canada, fifty times as much as it does in Europe, and between three hundred to two thousand times as much as it does in developing nations.

The copper IUD is the most widely used method of reversible birth control in the world, and its cost-effectiveness has been studied and confirmed in countless studies from multiple countries. That aspect of the research is not in dispute. What does merit investigation is the assumptions that have contributed to an apparent helplessness in America, a resignation to the inevitability that medical pricing should be constrained at all, even at the expense of massive externalities (outside costs). For example, only in the United States will you see a statement like, "IUD costs would need to exceed $10,500 per woman before the program would begin to cost the state more than future pregnancy costs."[2] That this is said to support the cost-effectiveness of a tiny piece of plastic and copper, and not as evidence towards the extravagance of medical costs in general is, quite frankly, bizarre. That cost-effectiveness research has been done on contraception for twenty years and not a single researcher has ever questioned why a piece of plastic and copper should cost nearly a thousand dollars is confirmation of what Dr. Richard Smith, previous editor of the prestigious medical journal BMJ, wrote: "[C]ompanies seem to get the results they want not by fiddling the results, which would be far too crude and possibly detectable by peer review, but rather **by asking the 'right' questions**."[3] (emphasis mine)

Despite this quite conspicuous absence, in recent years there has certainly been progress in minimizing healthcare costs in America. For example, research has consistently found that an investment in contraceptive access leads to savings due to the prevention of unplanned pregnancies and abortions. Despite my pointing out the absurd logic of calibrating contraceptive cost-effectiveness solely on birthing costs, there is no sound economic argument against increasing access to, or even subsidizing, effective contraceptives.

Further, now that the Affordable Care Act (ACA) requires that all health insurance plans cover one of each type in the Food and Drug Administration (FDA)-approved pharmacopeia of contraceptive methods, women's contraceptive choices in the United States might, for the first time in a long time, reflect their actual preferences instead of economic status. In that way, it may appear— and indeed it is my hope—that the central argument to the chapter, "In an IUDeal World," will appear dated and irrelevant to readers living in a modern America in which effective contraceptives are finally accessible to all American citizens.

But arguably the most important lessons that the economic

history of the IUD in America can teach us have not been solved. The ACA has focused almost entirely on the inefficiency of the private insurance market, a sector which has famously been described as, "an administrative monstrosity, a truly bizarre mélange of thousands of payers with payment systems that differ for no socially beneficial reason, as well as staggeringly complex public system with mindboggling administered prices and other rules expressing distinctions that can only be regarded as weird."[4] One of the most important contributions of the ACA is the medical loss ratio, which requires health insurance companies to spend 80-85% of the consumers' premium dollars they collect on actual medical care rather than overhead, marketing expenses, and profit. This law is meant to cut down on the "administrative monstrosity" aspect of the American private health insurance in-dustry, and has been described as the "true 'death panel' found in Obamacare"[5] in that if forces insurance companies to stop seek-ing ways to deny coverage and start serving their purported purpose of providing affordable healthcare. "Everyone wins," Forbes writer Rick Ungar has written, "except the for-profit health insurers."

However, despite its clear advantages, in a world in which all other industrialized nations attained universal health care coverage decades ago, trying to muster enthusiasm for a health care reform on the basis that it requires health insurance companies to spend money on providing health care, and bans them from denying coverage to the sick, is a bit like collecting crumbs and being told to call it a feast. Additionally, despite the progress the ACA has made towards addressing issues in the private health insurance industry, it has done nothing to combat the wasteful behaviors in the pharmaceutical industry. The ACA has instead provided the industry with millions of new customers while asking for no concessions in return. Of course, many would say that it's no secret that the pharmaceutical industry is massively lucrative, and that it doesn't logically follow that profitability alone is inherently problematic. After all, as the medical industry endeavors to solve increasingly complex or chronic health problems, research and development (R&D) costs must increase in tandem. The search for new medicine is by nature an incredibly costly process, and if big profits are necessary for an increase in R&D investment and innovation, profit-seeking in the pharmaceutical industry should be encouraged, not disdained.

This line of reasoning is only halfway accurate. It's true that large amounts of money often correlate with medical breakthroughs. The United States spends more money on medicine than any-where else in the world, and most—but not all[6]—researchers agree that it in turn produces the most breakthroughs as well. But the important thing to notice is that correlation is not causation, and we need not focus on input (how much money we spend) but rather, output (what we get back). When the question is reframed thusly, the evidence strongly suggests that the pharmaceutical industry does not produce in amounts that would be nearly proportionate to its remuneration.[7] That is to say, research indicates that the US spends considerably more money than any other country on pharmaceuticals, but produces only slightly more breakthroughs.

Further, an important component to the discussion of pharma-ceutical R&D development must acknowledge that no one really knows how much money it costs to develop new drugs. One well-traveled figure has placed the estimate at $802 million for the year 2000,[8] but that estimate has been criticized for its lack of transparency-and verifiability-in sources, its uncritical acceptance of industry-reported f igures, and inappropriate—if not blatantly dishonest—method of mathematical calculation.[9] On the sub-ject of the public's uncritical acceptance of the pharmaceutical industry's R&D cost claim, medical ethicist Donald Light has written:

> *"Industry executives, well supplied with facts and figures by the industry's global press network, awe audiences with staggering figures for the cost of a single trial, like tribal chieftains and their scribes who recount the mythic costs of a great victory in a remote pass where no outside witnesses saw the battle."[10]*

Speaking of "mythic costs", the inappropriate and dishonest method of calculation which discredits the $802 million estimate is that the figure was doubled by including the, "cost of capital," which is a term to describe hypothetical money a pharmaceutical firm could have made—but didn't—if they had devoted their energies elsewhere, such as in the stock market. This is often otherwise referred to as "opportunity cost." This method of calculation is appropriate to use in brainstorming, when a business is deciding between one of many courses of action, but for a R&D-heavy industry to cite unmade, hypothetical profits as a direct cost of operation is unreasonable, even unethical. Similarly, a Congressional Budget Office report has observed that federal tax credits given to pharmaceutical companies for R&D costs might encourage these companies to exaggerate their costs.[11] The fact is, "outside witnesses" don't even have an educated guess in regard to how much money it costs to develop a new treatment—a circumstance that is no doubt to the benefit of, and possibly intentionally perpetuated by, high-profit pharmaceutical companies.

Nonetheless, big money in medicine is not the problem. Linking medical finance directly to market performance is. As it currently stands, pharmaceutical companies are financially rewarded directly in proportion to the amount of drugs sold and the highest price they can sell them for, which results in priorities that are skewed towards rapid price inflation, ruthless marketing, and a myriad of decidedly un-Hippocratic perverse incentives. In order to ensure that pharmaceutical companies earn a return on the amount the claim to have invested, the state has been turned from guardians of consumer safety to guardians of corporate profit, which in turn requires unnecessary sacrifices that begin at Americans' freedom of consumer choice, but can potentially extend as far as sacrifices in safety. What's more, most Americans are completely ignorant of these factors and will undoubtedly find such claims hyperbolic, unless they continue reading and allow me to defend them.

Because the significance of this investigation is primarily in what the IUD reveals about the US health system in general, I have no doubt that every American—regardless of contraceptive need—can find elements of this book highly relevant. However, in my attempt to adequately justify my claims, I've also provided sufficient detail about the IUD that I have no doubt that this is not the most exciting book ever written. The central argument will doubtless be more compelling to those who read the book in its entirety, but chapters can also be skimmed or skipped. What follows is a breakdown of the central ideas defended in each chapter, so that readers can decide whether to take the following chapter arguments on authority, or read the appropriate chapters and notes to seek support for the following statements:

**Chapter 1:** The copper IUD is one of the best contraceptive options available to women today. The copper IUD is highly utilized outside of the US and strangely scarcely used within it.

**Chapter 2:** Financial interests combined with FDA laxity led to an unsafe IUD hitting the American market in the 1970's, which subsequently posed a problem to public health. Consequential reticence on the part of consumers and doctors, as well as economic concerns on the part of providers, resulted in several IUD makers pulling out of the American IUD market. The IUD became temporarily unavailable to America women, and upon its return to America the IUD began a dramatic upward price trajectory that continues to this day.

**Chapter 3:** The copper IUD, like most pharmaceuticals, is very cheap to produce. The price Americans pay for the device is significantly higher than in other countries, and has inflated to a point where it is unaffordable to most Americans. Prohibitive expense strongly contributes to the relative underutilization of the IUD in the United States.

**Chapter 4:** Allowing the IUD to be priced out of access to the women who have the highest need for it has resulted in externalities which cost the American taxpayers some $10 billion dollars in a single year, and perpetuates a circumstance of inequality of opportunity.

**Chapter 5:** Monopoly power and FDA enforcement allow pharmaceutical companies to charge American consumers far more for pharmaceuticals than what is charged in other countries, even for identical products from the same manufacturer. What results is that ordinary consumer actions are criminalized, and the FDA shifts its role from safeguarding people to becoming guardians of profit.

**Chapter 6:** Monopoly pricing for pharmaceuticals combined with failed mechanisms of pricing controls in America have caused high prices in both the private and public sectors. I explain these mechanisms, how this has occurred, and why low prices are institutionally made impossible to obtain in America.

**Chapter 7:** The IUD reveals one of many instances in which perpetuating a monopoly-controlled pharmaceutical industry has resulted in grossly perverted incentives. As the largest pharmaceutical market in the world, Americans bear the responsibility for the perversion of the pharmaceutical industry, but there are options to realign incentives while maintaining profits and private industry. However, even ardent proponents of this strategy have low expectations that it will be implemented in America in the current political climate.

**Conclusion:** The questions that are asked dictate the answers that are received. The parameters of inquiry have been defined in such a way that dishonestly frames the public debate, and consequently Americans have been misled about the full extent of their options, and even own opinions. It's time for American citizens to ask their own, better questions.

Readers may be disappointed to find that this book does not finish with a specified plan of action. Notice that this book is not entitled, "What's wrong with pharmaceuticals in America and what you can do about it." There are two reasons for that. The first is, I found many things that were wrong with the state of America's management of the pharmaceutical industry (or lack thereof), but I don't flatter myself to claim that I know what can be done about it. But one does not need to know the conclusion prior to beginning the process of inquiry. My intention was to synthesize and compile information in such a way that no one has yet, in hopes to facilitate action moving in the right direction. Before Americans can be expected to make any changes, they need to first realize that their circumstances are unique, and therefore not an immutable fact of life, but rather the result of very specific, and changeable, circumstances. This has only occurred on a very sporadic and superficial level.

This change will not be easy. The road is long and unforgiving, there is no map, and the street signs are misleading. There is a reason for that. Many Americans have increasingly felt a sense of disempowerment regarding the direction of the country, and with good reason. In 2014 researchers from Princeton and Northwestern University analyzed public opinion and policy changes over nearly two thousand issues between the years of 1981 and 2002, and reported that:

> *"[E]conomic elites and organized groups representing business interests have substantial independent impacts on US government policy, while **average citizens and mass-based interest groups have little or no independent influence**. The results provide substantial support for theories of Economic Elite Domination and for theories of Biased Pluralism, but not for theories of Majoritarian Electoral Democracy or Majoritarian Pluralism."[12]* (emphasis mine)

In other words, what money wants matters a lot, and what people want matters a little. The researchers did note that while American voters do not have nearly as much impact on American policy as business interests do, average American voters do get what they want approximately 64% percent of the time. However, this is largely because in those cases what the average voters want is the same as what the elites and special interests want—a phenomenon the researchers dubbed, "democracy by coincidence."

The researchers further specified that, "ordinary citizens get what they want from government only when they happen to agree with elites or interest groups that are really calling the shots." By contrast, in the remaining incidences in which average Americans want something other than what is desired by the elites or special interest groups:

> "The estimated impact of average citizens' preferences drops precipitously, to a **non-significant, near-zero level**. ..Not only do ordinary citizens not have uniquely substantial power over policy decisions; **they have little or no independent influence on policy at all**." (emphasis mine)

Perhaps a good example of this beguiling "democracy by co-incidence" is a comparison of the speed that at which pure grassroots issues which lack significant corporate intervention— such as the decriminalization of marijuana or increase in marriage equality for homosexuals—can proceed relatively rapidly in America, compared to issues which, if successful, would result in a significant loss of corporate profits—for example, gun control, healthcare reform, or even Americans obtaining the right to purchase equivalent medicines from abroad. It's enough to inspire fantasies about the speed of problem-solving that could occur if the absence of special-interest-intervention.

Consequently, the aim of this book is not to advocate a particular solution, but rather give concrete evidence to contribute to the national discussion of the problem. To that end, the economic history of the intrauterine device in America is not a case-in-point but rather a case study.

I first started researching this subject for very personal reasons. After I found out that the copper IUD can provide a decade of safe contraception, I wanted to know why I had never even heard of it, and had spent years using contraceptives with potentially dangerous side effects. Also, even though I privately suspected I was asking a Very Stupid Question, I wanted to know what it was that I didn't understand about plastic and copper that justified its high price. Most sources seemed to regard the price tag as unworthy of discussion, yet an online magazine article with a uniquely candid quote from a frustrated doctor let me know that maybe I wasn't excessively naïve in my curiosity:

> "'It's absolute highway robbery that these companies charge so much,' [Dr. Eve] Espey says. 'If you went to Home Depot and got the raw materials for a copper IUD, it would cost less than 5 cents.' And the hormones don't contribute much more to the cost, she adds."[13]

Some time after, I found myself reading news accounts of doctors being charged with fraud, misbranding smuggling, and even risking prison time over purchasing IUDs from across national borders. Intuitively that seemed an excessively harsh regulatory response, but still I looked for a good reason to justify the system as it was. At the point that I found myself on the telephone with an Indian IUD manufacturer and hearing that they, and many of their peers, are able to and interested in providing equivalent, low-cost, pharmaceuticals to the American market, but are afraid of lobbying from powerful global pharmaceutical juggernauts—it was clear at that point that this was a national discussion that needed to take place.

Even so, when I first started writing my initial draft in late 2013, I thought it was possible that I was wasting my time, unhealthily preoccupied with a problem for which the solution was looming. After all, the ACA required that all FDA-approved contraceptives be covered in all health insurance plans, and Medicines 360, a nonprofit pharmaceutical company, was in the process of developing an IUD which they promised to offer American women at a low price. Even better, the state of Maine had just legalized parallel importation of the equivalents of FDA-approved drugs from Canada, the UK, Australia, and New Zealand. It appeared that the hundred thousand percent markup of a sterilized piece of plastic and copper was notable, certainly, but not likely to be a persistent problem in the United States. A temporary fissure in an otherwise functional system.

However, since finishing my initial draft, a federal judge has overturned Maine's victory and once again forbidden parallel importation of cheaper, identical drugs from abroad. Copper IUD prices have gone up from $754 to $932. The House has voted to defund or otherwise delay the ACA over 50 times. The Supreme Court has alarmingly ruled that though corporations can neither think nor feel, they are nonetheless entitled to protected religious beliefs, and those "beliefs" can be used to deny contraceptive coverage those employed by the corporation. What's more, in the face of it all, a woman has been sentenced to 20 years of imprisonment for the conflicting charges of "neglect of a dependent," and "feticide" in a case with little evidence that either had occurred. It has long been known that the power to control her reproductive cycle is crucial in order for a woman to have economic freedom, but even in my deepest pit of pessimism, I never would have predicted that in such a short period of time, America would devolve into a place where women would both be experiencing increasing hurdles to control their reproductive cycles at the same time that inability to do so could literally result in imprisonment.

Furthermore, this rapid deterioration of rights has highlighted a flummoxing circumstance in which Americans will placidly observe an attack on the government's authority to wield any control over corporate interests—often masked by cries for a "small government" that will not overstep its bounds—but will not comment on the relative lack of silence on issues which actually do threaten a shuffle from the safe boundaries of democracy towards the iron walls of authoritarianism. Though it is hyperbolic to describe either as such, a government which imprisons a woman for her poor response to a miscarriage is far closer to authoritarianism than a government which provides health insurance to its people is to communism. Yet the latter is an idea which carries more weight in modern America, particularly among politicians. How is it possible that Americans —once so proud of their independence —have paradoxically acquiesced to the philosophy of diminished governmental authority only on the issues which could significantly provide them with an enhanced quality of life and the power to wring pro-consumer concessions from corporations—for example to provide affordable health insurance or negotiate lower drug prices on their behalf— but will not raise their own voices against the silence on issues that actually give credence to fears of encroaching tyranny—for example increased militarization of police forces and criminalizing the natural functions of the female body?

In reference to Purvi Patel's 20-year prison sentence, Lynn M. Paltrow has written:

> *"If a woman suffers an unexplained miscarriage or stillbirth, would the fact that she had previously searched for information about using medications like misoprostol to end a pregnancy be used against her? In the Patel case,*

*the state had no physical proof that Patel had actually taken*

*—or even purchased—any medication, apart from text messages*

*allegedly discussing these matters.(For the record, the state*

*similarly had no actual proof that the fetus had been born alive,*

*relying instead on a scientifically invalid and widely discredited*

*"float test" to persuade the jury otherwise.)*

*What the Patel case demonstrates is that both women who*

*have abortions and those who experience pregnancy loss may*

*now be subject to investigation, arrest, public trial and*

*incarceration. Indeed, Patel has consistently said that she*

*experienced a miscarriage that she, like most women in this*

*situation, was unprepared to handle. Pregnancy loss is not*

*uncommon: some 15-20 percent of all known pregnancies end*

*in miscarriage; one percent of pregnancies—approximately*

*26,000 each year—result in stillbirth. Following the Patel case,*

*however, any miscarriage or stillbirth could be investigated*

*as feticide (an "illegal" self-abortion)."[14]*

There is, of course, a consistent theme connecting the changes in American life which seem to happen very quickly, and those which never seen to go anywhere, despite popular opinion among the constituency: changes in American policy can be quite easily predicted by whether or not special interests stand to lose, or gain, significant amounts of money. There's money to be made in extending marriage rights to more individuals. There's money to be made in the creation of a legal marijuana industry. The money that a largely-privatized prison industry stands to lose in decriminalizing marijuana can be made in finding new offense—for example, miscarriages—to criminalize. There's significant amounts of money to be lost in addressing why Americans receive poorer health care for higher prices, why monopolists are unhindered in setting American pharmaceutical prices far above the global norm, and prohibiting American consumers from purchasing identical- sometimes safer-products from abroad. In modern American political discourse, it's never really about the philosophy of a big or small government—it's always about big or small profit margins.

Americans need to take a close look at the copper IUD and what it is, and what it has to show them about what they've come to accept. It is literally just a sterilized a piece of plastic with copper wrapped around it. The Tcu380A copper IUD which is available in America for nearly $1,000 is no better than the Tcu380A which is available in the United Kingdom for $20, or in developing nations for less than $1. There are no complicated hormones embedded inside, no high-tech spermicidal lasers that would justify charging Americans thousands of times more than the standard global price. There is nothing for an average layperson to be ill-equipped to understand. I dare say that if American consumers can look at a device this simple—a tiny object with literally nothing to hide—and not see it for evidence of opportunistic corporate abuse of power, this is worse than the parable of the emperor with no clothes. This circumstance more closely resembles an emperor conducting a tantric orgy in a public square, to a citizenry that responds with rave reviews of his exquisite fashion sense. It's quite clear that America does not yet have the medical system is wants, but I dare say that if even America's most critical watchdogs can see women's rights being diminished by the artificial scarcity of a thousand-dollar sterilized piece of plastic and copper, and think that the circumstances are inevitable or in any way reasonable, America already has the medical system it deserves.

# NOTES

[1] Docteur (2008)

[2] Rodriguez (2010)

[3] Smith (2005)

[4] Aaron (2003)

[5] Ungar (2011)

[6] See Light & Lexchin deconstruct the myth that US pharmaceutical expenditures result in more break-throughs, and that countries which spend less are taking advantage of US gains: Foreign free riders and the high price of US medicines. BMJ: British Medical Journal 331.7522 (2005)

[7] The Congressional Budget Office (2006) has observed that, "Continued growth in R&D spending has appeared to have little effect on the pace at which new drugs are developed," and that, "Measured by the number of drugs approved per dollar of R&D, the innovative performance of the drug industry appears to have declined." Others have criticized the industry more directly, nothing that over the past few decades pharmaceutical income and purported R&D spending has increased considerably, but pharmaceutical innovation has continued at a constant rate (Boldrin, 2008) (Light, 2012).

[8]     DiMasi (2003)

[9]     Light (2011) and the CBO (2006) have observed that half of the cost included in the $802 million estimate is not a direct expense but rather "cost of capital."

While the CBO report did not criticize DiMasi for using opportunity cost in the calculation, it did observe that federal tax credits given to pharmaceutical companies for R&D costs might encourage these companies to exaggerate their costs, though the report acknowledged it did not have direct evidence of this having occurred (but how could it, without a pharmaceutical firm revealing its financial books?)

[10]    Light (2011)

[11]    Congressional Budget Office (2006)

[12]    Gilens et al. (2014)

[13]    Couzin-Frankel (2011)

[14]    Paltrow (2015)

# PART I:

## CONTRACEPTIVE SECURITY THREATENED

*"Contraceptive Security is said to exist when people are able to choose, obtain, and use high-quality contraceptives whenever they need them."*

Sarley, David, et al. Options for contraceptive procurement: lessons learned from Latin America and the Caribbean. 2006

# CHAPTER 1
## THE GOLD STANDARD IS MADE OF COPPER

*"The optimal IUD choice has important public health implications as it concerns millions of women worldwide."*

Kulier et al. Copper containing, framed intra-uterine devices for contraception (Review). 2008

The Center for Disease Control estimates that 98% of all American women use contraceptives within their lifetimes, and at any given moment approximately 60% of American women of reproductive age are using some form of birth control.[1] There remains a need for increased use of reliable contraceptives, as evidenced by the rate that approximately 50% of all US pregnancies every year are unintended[2] and nearly half of those to women who were using birth control at the time of conception.[3] Though the abortion rate in the United States has been steadily declining for the past thirty years, approximately 20% of all pregnancies still end in an induced abortion, to an amount in excess of 1 million abortions per year. [4] In addition to reducing incidences of unwanted pregnancies and abortions in the interest of the public good, the US has an economic interest in investing in contraceptive access, as advocates have routinely estimated that every dollar that goes to family planning leads to at least three times the amount in government savings.[5] Additionally, 65% of unintended births are paid for by Medicaid,[6] which amounts to Medicaid paying for approximately one million unintended births a year, with annual cost to taxpayers of approximately $10 billion.[7]

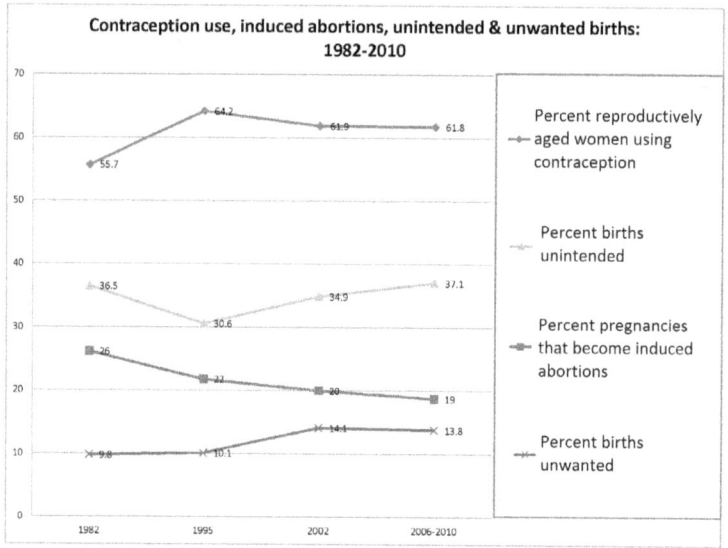

*Figure 1. Sources: CDC National Survey of Family Growth, CDC Vital Statistics. See Appendix A.*

Of the methods of reversible birth control available, long-acting reversible contraceptives (LARCs) such as intrauterine devices (IUDs) are among the most reliable. Typical-use failure rates of two IUDs— ParaGard® and Mirena® —are 0.6% and 0.2% respectively, compared to 9% with the pill or 18% with the condom.[8] In simplistic terms, that means that for every 1,000 IUD users only 2-6 of them will get pregnant, compared to approximately 90 to 180 pill and condom users. Part of what makes IUDs and other LARCs so exceptionally effective is that they remove the human factor. Contrary to pills and shots which require following a schedule, or condoms, which must be kept on hand and used properly during intercourse, LARCs do not require any action on the part of the user-they are a "set it and forget it" type of contraception. Additionally, copper IUDs have very few contraindications, meaning they can be used by almost any woman. [9] Side effects include heavier or more painful menstrual periods, but those side effects usually fade after the first few months as the body becomes accustomed to the copper, and give way to a decade of effortless, reliable contraception.[10]

In 2007 an estimated 162 million women used IUDs worldwide, constituting approximately 23% of all global contraceptive users in over 100 countries.[11] The United Nations reported that in 2009 the IUD was the most widely-used reversible contraceptive method in the world among women who are married or in a union.[12] The majority of IUD users are located in China,[13] but the contraceptive is also widely used in Europe, comprising as many as 23% of contraceptive users in Norway, 23% in Finland, and 21% in France.[14]

In particular, the TCu380A copper IUD—which is known under the brand name ParaGard® in the United States— has been placed on the World Health Organization's list of essential medicines for contraceptive security, and categorized as the, "preferred device... on the basis of its efficacy, safety and long history of use."[15] In 2008 the Cochrane Collaboration performed a meta-analysis in which they evaluated 35 trials of over 48,000 women and concluded that the copper-bearing T-frame IUDs such as the TCu380A and the related TCu380S are, "the most effective, have the longest duration of action and are the IUDs of choice."[16]

The general consensus of reproductive research and public policy is that the TCu380A is the considered the, "international gold standard."[17]

A note on the taxonomy of intrauterine devices: The general term "IUD" could be used to refer to any type of contraceptive device which is placed inside the uterus. Currently In the United States there are only three IUDs available on the market—ParaGard®, Mirena®, and Skyla™, offered by solely two manufacturers—but a fourth IUD from a third manufacturer has just received FDA-approval, though at the point of this writing, it has not yet hit the American market. Throughout the rest of the world there is a much wider variety in generic versions of the devices Americans can purchase, as well as variations unavailable in the US, including frameless devices.

Copper IUDs such as ParaGard® derive their function through copper ions being released from the device, and are non-hormonal. In contrast, the Mirena®, Skyla™, and the brand-new Liletta™, function by releasing the hormone levonorgestrel, and are sometimes referred to as an LNG-IUS (levonorgestrel intrauterine system), but usually only when a distinction is being made between hormonal and non-hormonal IUDs. In most instances, such as in research literature or the Center for Disease Control (CDC) National Survey of Family Growth (NSFG), the term "IUD" is a blanket term used to refer to any of the related devices.

Though the copper IUD and the hormonal LNG-IUS share many similarities in effectiveness and cost, they are not identical products. For example, because the LNG-IUS releases hormones it has several distinct side effects, such as amenoria (lack of menstruation), which could either be a benefit or a drawback to the device, depending on the subjective experience of the user. Additionally, hormone-releasing IUDs need to be replaced every 3-5 years, but the copper-bearing TCu380A is approved up 10-12 years, and there is evidence that it could continue to function for as many as 20 years.[18] Thus, depending on the context or purpose, the copper IUD and the LNG-IUS may be referred to collectively and are in some ways near equivalents, but they are not the same.

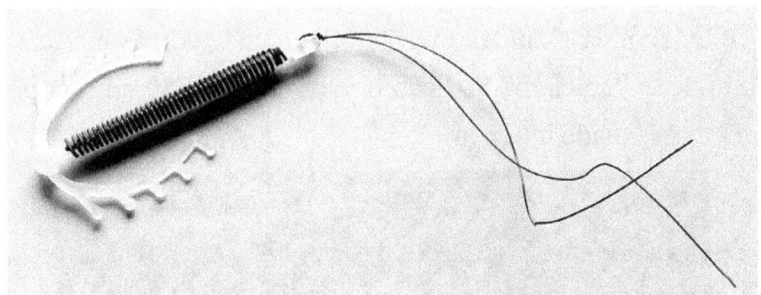

*Figure 2: The Multiload CU 250. Image courtesy of Aung via Wikimedia Commons.*

Within the specific classification of a "copper IUD" there is also a fair amount of variety. The most common frame shape is the T, but there are other shapes, such as the Lippes Loop, which has an S shape, or the Multiload, the shape of which somewhat crudely resembles a crustacean. Names for varying IUD models tend to have a number, which refers to the surface area of copper in the device. For example, the TCu380A has approximately $380mm^2$ of exposed copper, which is believed to be the optimal amount.[19] Devices with lower amounts of copper, such as the MLCu-250 (a Multiload model with $250mm^2$ copper) tend to have reduced side effects-less cramping and bleeding in the first few months of use -but they are also less effective than the TCu380A, with fewer recommended years of use.

The TCu380A copper IUD was developed in the United States by the nonprofit organization The Population Council, and is now made by multiple manufacturers all over the world.

However, in the United States it is currently only made available through Israel-based Teva Pharmaceutical Industries LTD, under the brand name ParaGard®. Throughout the literature ParaGard® is referred to interchangeably as both the TCu380A and the CuT 380A. As such, references to the TCu380A could refer either specifically to ParaGard® or more generally to any equivalent device by another manufacturer, but the registered name refers to the branded "ParaGard" and can only refer to a 380 mm$^2$ copper T IUD that is made by Teva.

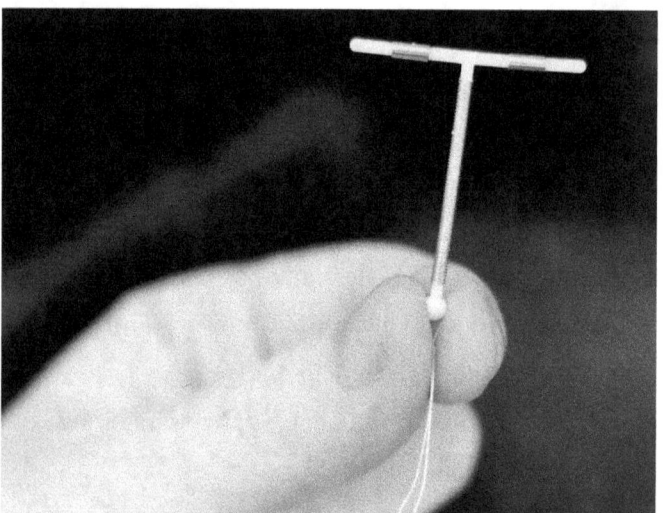

*Figure 3: The TCU380A copper IUD. Image courtesy of Florian Blümm.*

Though US citizens only have access to Teva's ParaGard®, worldwide there are several manufacturers of generic and branded TCu380As. For example in Europe there is the Flexi-T 380, T-Safe 380A, TT380 Slimline, UT 380, and the Neo-Safe T380, among others. Branded and generic products are then registered with a country's institutional authorities, which will determine in which country they can be sold. It would be illegal for a doctor to purchase an IUD from another country and then insert it in the United States, even if it is an identical device. This prohibition can even extend to devices from the same manufacturer. For example the Mirena® LNG-IUS is exclusively provided in the United States by Bayer AG, a German pharmaceutical company. Yet, purchasing a Mirena® IUD from a non-US supply chain constitutes the illegal importation of "foreign" products, whereas purchasing from an approved supplier is legal and not considered "foreign". The same is true for all pharmaceuticals, which is why the state of Maine has recently embarked upon the evidently quixotic quest to obtain the right for its residents to obtain identical drugs from outside the American supply chain.[20] This restriction is difficult to enforce with online pharmacies, but easily enforced in the case of an IUD because it has to be inserted by a qualified doctor, nurse, or midwife. By inserting a foreign IUD a healthcare professional would be putting him or herself at a great deal of risk, which will be described in further detail in later chapters.

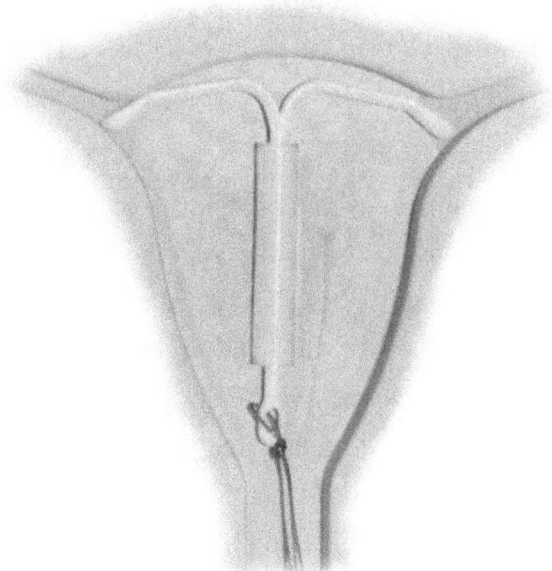

*Figure 4: The Mirena LNG-IUS in place. Image courtesy of Hic et nunc via Wikimedia Commons.*

Within the United States, interest in IUDs has been steadily increasing since the change in millennia, as indicated by increased rates of current use. Additionally, there has been an increase in volume of research papers concluding that in an increased in IUD usage would have a large impact in reducing unexpected or unwanted pregnancies and associated costs.[21] Despite the high upfront cost of the device, IUDs have frequently been described as among the most cost-effective methods of birth control,[22] with the potential for many years' use to mitigate the high upfront costs, as well as calculated savings from prevented unplanned pregnancies. In order to better display the relative savings, the ParaGard® official website, until recently,

[23] provided a pricing chart indicating that a new ParaGard® IUD cost approximately $754 (not including doctor visit or insertion fees). This price may appear high in the first year, but this amount is dwarfed by the cost of a decade's worth of other contraceptives. For example, the pill was used by 17% of reproductively-aged women in 2006-2010, which, according to the ParaGard® pricing chart, could have cost of $11,512.80 per person per decade.

A further testament to the high level of trust the medical community places in IUDs is the increased rate of IUD use among physicians, with rates 5-10 times higher than in the general public.[24] Despite this strong recommendation, IUD usage rates in America are potentially the lowest in the developed world, and are currently only used by approximately 7% of contracepting American women. Many researchers have noted the relative underutilization of the IUD and asked: if IUDs are such a panacea to public health, why are they so scarce in America?

# NOTES

[1]     Mosher (2010) pg 18 and pg 21

[2]     Mosher, William (2012) pg 1

[3]     Guttmacher Institute, Facts on unintended pregnancy in the United States, In Brief, 2013. Hubacher (2002) and (2011) note the same, with estimates of just over or just under 50%. Mosher (2012) reports that 40% of all unintended births occur to women who report having been using birth control at the time of conception.

[4]     The chart on pg 9 of Ventura (2012) reports total numbers of pregnancies, births, induced abortions, and fetal losses, and then rates of these events per thousand women

[5]     Various estimates on cost savings attributable to contraception will be discussed in further detail in chapter, In an IUDeal World.

[6]     Mosher (2012) pg 13, 24.

[7]     Monea (2011)

[8]     Barot (2013) pg 2

[9]     World Health Organization (WHO) 2010 reports, "The IUD is safe and suitable for nearly all women including adolescents and women over 40, women who have just

had an abortion or miscarriage as long as there is no infection, women who are breastfeeding, women who have had pelvic inflammatory disease and are currently free from infection, and women who are infected with HIV on antiretroviral therapy and clinically well. If, however, a woman has a very high individual risk of having gonorrhea or chlamydia at the time of insertion, or if she has AIDS and is not on antiretroviral therapy and not clinically well, she should not have an IUD inserted." (pg 10)

Contraindications listed in the Encyclopedia of Birth Control (Bullough 2001) include: copper allergy, Wilson's disease, a pelvic infection, a history of ectopic pregnancy, a gynecological bleeding disorder, malignancy in the genital tract, uterine abnormalities, or current pregnancy (pps 152-153).

[10]    Kulier (2008) reports, "Increased or prolonge vaginal bleeding has been described as the most common side-effect…and could be related to the copper content of the IUD, therefore raising concern that this may decrease the tolerability and compliance with high copper content devices. Smaller devices with less copper content aim to minimise side effects and to provide an alternative for women with smaller sized uterus, but may be less effective. Other side effects reported are abdominal pain, especially during menstruation, and vaginal discharge" (pg 3).

[11]    World Health Organization (WHO) (2010) pg 10

[12]    UN (2009)

[13]    Wen (2010) reports 70% of all IUD users are Chinese.

[14]    Clifton (2008) reports that the IUD is used by 1.9% of married women using family planning in America, but

14.2% in Mexico, 39.6% in China, 17.3% in France,

8.8% in Austria, and 6% in Switzerland and the U.K. These estimates do not include unmarried women. Clifton's numbers differ from a UN report (2009), potentially because Clifton only includes married women in the estimates and the U.N. report extends to women who are unmarried but in a union. Sonfield (2007) reports as many as 27% of Norwegian and 21% of all Swedish contraceptive users use IUDs.

[15]    World Health Organization (WHO) (2010) pg 12

[16]    Kulier (2008) pg 2

[17]    Black (2011).

[18]     Sivin (2007), Nelson (2011)

[19]    Kulier (2008) reports "Our review has demonstrated that the frame and amount and position of copper all play a part in performance. The T-shaped devices, when carrying a surface area of 380mm2 of copper performed better than other contenders. In general, the comparative analyses suggest higher effectiveness and similar side-effect profile with high copper IUDs compared to low copper ones although some variability exists in different comparisons." (pg 10)

[20]    See Hemphill (2013), PBS (2014), Farwell (2015), and Wight (2015), to follow some of the back-and-forth on this issue.

[21]     See Hubacher (2002), Blumenthal (2011), Hubacher (2011), MacIsaac (2007), Moskosky (2011), Sonfield (2007), Trussell (1995), (1997a), (1997b), (2009), (2012), Rodriguez (2010), among many others. Needless to say, it's a commonly held belief. Some researchers have essentially built their research careers around finding different ways to come to this conclusion.

[22]     Blumenthal (2011), Finer (2012), Foster (2009), Gariepy (2011), Rodriguez (2010), Secura (2010), Trussell (1995), (1997a), (1997b), (2009), (2012), Chiou (2003), ACOG (2012), Nelson (2011) among many, many others. If you can find me a research paper written between 1995 and 2013 that mentions IUDs and does not mention their cost-effectiveness when potential for long term use is considered, I'll refund you the cost of this book.

[23]     The ParaGard® pricing chart was accessed on December 13, 2013 and for most of 2014 was available at: http://www.paragard.com/how-do-i-get-it/cost-chart.aspx. However, by January 31, 2015 the comparative chart had been removed and the price of ParaGard® had increased from $754 to $932, now sans the pricing comparison.

[24]     MacIsaac (2007) reports, "Women physicians have consistently used IUDs more than age- and income-matched women, even before the marketing of the levonorgestrel intrauterine system (LNG IUS). In the 1995 'Women's Physician Health Study,' approximately 1% of women in the general population used IUDs, whereas 5% of female physicians and 9% of female obstetrician/gynecologists used them."

# CHAPTER 2
## THE IUD GOES MIA

*"Because of legal and economic problems peculiar to the United States, the most commonly used IUDs are no longer available to US women. These problems, fortunately, do not exist outside the United States."*

Ramirez et al. The Ending of IUD Sales in the United States: What Are the International Implications? 1987

I t's difficult for today's youth to appreciate the full histori- cal importance of the advent of modern birth control, which the CDC has called one of the, "Ten Great Public Health Achievements of the 20th Century."[1] Multiple researchers have commented that after the birth control pill was developed in the 1960's, women could, for the first time in history, invest in their education and pursue career goals with a reasonable expectation that their plans would not be disrupted by an unplanned pregnancy. [2] Widespread use of the birth control pill also led to women marrying later in life, allowing them to set firm educational and economic foundations prior to starting families. Pointing out the low effectiveness of the birth control pill compared to methods available today should not detract from how absolutely revolutionary its development was for women in the 1960's, and that it likely contributed more to women's equality than any amount of marches, demonstrations, or protests.

However, in the 1970's doctors started to raise concerns about a connection between the birth control pill and an increase in blood clots. Unwilling to once again be constrained by biology, women sought an alternative birth control method, and interest in IUDs increased. At the time, intrauterine devices were a very recent and lightly-tested invention, and were not even under the jurisdiction of the FDA. The first copper-bearing IUD had only just been invented in 1969 by Drs. J. Zipper and H. Tatum, who observed that winding copper filament around the vertical stem of a T-shaped device increased its effectiveness as well as its lifespan. At that point the mechanisms of the copper IUD were not understood, but it is now believed that copper IUDs prevent pregnancy by releasing copper ions from the device which stimulate an inflammatory reaction that kills sperm, renders the uterus inhospitable to fertilization, and also creates an intrauterine environment that is hostile to implantation.[3] Because copper IUDs can be used as emergency contraception for up to five days after intercourse, their "Plan B" utility has given rise to a rumor that copper IUDs cause abortions, but in fact what they do is prevent conception from happening in the first place.

Shortly after their introduction to the market, interest in IUDs rose rapidly and by 1976, 2.4 million American women were using IUDs.[4] As demand for the devices increased, so did potential suppliers. One person hoping to cash in on the burgeoning

IUD market was Hugh Davis with the AH Robins Company, and their new product: the Dalkon Shield. Part of the secret to the Dalkon's rapid rise to success is that Davis intentionally targeted birth control pill users, exploiting increasing fears regarding the safety of the birth control pill.

"Never in history have so many individuals taken such potent drugs with so little information as to actual potential hazards," claimed Hugh Davis upon the evening news.[5] Davis's smear campaign against the birth control pill was a staggering display of hypocrisy and blatant scramble for market share, as his product, the Dalkon Shield, was virtually untested itself and later revealed to be especially hazardous. Nonetheless, Davis's advertising and propaganda campaign succeeded in directing women towards the Dalkon Shield, and by the early 80's the company claimed to have sold over 2 million devices.[6]

Almost immediately after the device's introduction, Dalkon's distributor, AH Robins, was made aware that the complications and pregnancy rates for the Dalkon Shield were much higher than advertised, but chose to neither warn the public nor recall the device. By the company's own estimates over 90,000 women were eventually injured by the Dalkon Shield.[7] By the mid 1970's the medical community began to observe a high number of serious complications and even deaths among Dalkon users, but it was not until ten years and multiple lawsuits had passed that AH Robbins issued a product recall and subsequently filed for bankruptcy in 1985.[8]

At the time, Louise Tyler, then medical director of the Planned Parenthood Federation of America, remarked that, "It is a disastrous situation when women are denied use of the

IUD because of today's litigious climate and a company's inability to retain insurance coverage."[9] Tyler was right to lament the insurance issues which rendered all IUDs guilty by association and inaccessible to American women, but absolutely wrong in referring to the Dalkon lawsuits and the litigious climate as a "disastrous situation." The Dalkon manufacturers knew that it could cause injury and death to consumers, yet because IUDs were not yet subject to FDA approval at the time, there was little mechanism but American litigiousness to effectively stop the manufacturers from knowingly peddling a dangerous product to unknowing consumers.

Though these incidents were particular to the Dalkon Shield, the Dalkon disaster made many people very skittish about IUDs in general, and citing hardship, two makers of three types of IUDs stopped marketing the products in the United States. These IUDs were safe and effective, but companies were, "unwilling to expose the entire assets of the corporation for the sake of products, which, though medically safe, were vulnerable to litigation while adding little to corporate revenues."[10] Due to Dalkon litigation and insurer paranoia, it became nearly impossible for IUD providers to obtain liability insurance in the 1980's.[11] Additionally, many American clinics either stopped carrying IUDs or otherwise recommended that IUD-using women remove their device at the next office visit.[12] In the United States, an unprecedented "removal of virtually an entire method from the contraceptive array,"[13] ensued for the following years, and by 1986 not a single IUD was available on the US market.

In explaining the why the United States is the only country in which the IUD has performed such a disappearing act, the Encyclopedia of Birth Control reports:

*"A major reason for the difference between the use of IUDs in the United States and the rest of the world is that the United States is practically alone among countries of the world in relying almost totally on private enterprise for its pharmaceuticals even though much of the research is paid for by the government. Obviously, private pharmaceutical companies want to sell IUDs for a profit. Because only a small percentage of American women used the device—approximately seven percent in 1982-83—and because IUDs are long lasting, profits from an IUD after the initial adoption were modest. The Lippes IUD, for example, cost only a few pennies to manufacture, and though it required the services of a physician to insert, few drug companies would gain any profit from selling it, and it simply ceased to be distributed in the United States."[14]*

The IUD did not make its tentative return to the United States until 1988 when Gyno Pharma Inc., then-makers of ParaGard®, decided to give the American market another try. The TCu380A had in fact been FDA approved and sold abroad for several years before coming home to the US. The copper IUD returned to an American market very different from the one it had left. For one thing, consumer demand had decreased considerably. In 1976 the CDC reported that approximately 6% of married women and 9% of separated, widowed, or divorced women used IUDs (it should be noted that because data on never-married IUD users was not reported in the study, IUD usage rates might have in fact been much higher).[15] By 1988, the percent of women using IUDs had plummeted to 1.2%.[16]

Another noteworthy difference, likely related to difficulty obtaining insurance, the cost of newly-required FDA approval, or both, was a dramatic increase in price. Prior to the Dalkon fiasco IUDs could be purchased for approximately $25—roughly equivalent $50 US dollars when inflation-adjusted to the year 2013. [17] Only a handful of years later, in 1991 the TCu380 had multiplied several times over to a price of $184, or something over $300 when adjusted for inflation.[18] Both of these indirect consequences of the Dalkon Shield—low usage rates and rapid price inflation—would continue to characterize the IUD in America for the following decades.

# NOTES

[1]      CDC.gov: http://www.cdc.gov/about/history/teng-pha.htm

[2]      Bailey (2012) compared data for women who came of age before the birth control pill hit the market compared to women who were approximately 20 years old when the FDA approved the pill for contraception in 1960, and found that early access to the pill contributed to more investment in human capital (ie college education, career) which led to the fraction of women in professional or managerial jobs being twice as high for the latter group than the former. By age 50, women who had early access to the pill earned approximately 8% more than their slightly older counterparts. The Testimony of Guttmacher Institute (2011) pg 6 also contains a summary of research related to the connection between the birth control pill and changes in women's lives in the 1960's.

[3]      Kulier et al. (2008) pg 2

[4]      Ford (1978)

[5]      Takeshita (2004) pg 70

[6]      Takeshita (2004) pg 75

[7]      Takeshita (2004) pg 76

[8]      Takeshita (2004) pg 145

[9]      Takeshita (2004), pg 78

[10]     Takeshita (2004), pg 77

[11]     Forrest (1986) and Ramirez (1987)

[12]     Forrest (1986)

[13]     Forrest (1986)

[14]     Bullough (2001)

[15]     Ford (1978)

[16]     Mosher (1990)

[17]     Ramirez (1987)

[18]     Trussell (1995)

# CHAPTER 3

## How Many Pennies Does it Take to Make an IUD?

*"We know IUDs are a more effective contraceptive option for many women, so we want to offer them as broadly as possible... But the up-front cost—anywhere from $200 to $400 each through 340B—is just too much for many clients and providers to bear."*

Karen Ford Manza, CEO of the Arizona Family Planning Council, 2010[1]

*"The copper IUD costs up to six times as much as the steel ring to produce (22 US cents vs 4 US cents per device)..."*

John Maurice. Progress in Reproductive Health Research. 2002

Ever since the return of IUDs in America researchers have broadly described IUDs as a wise expenditure in public health funds. In the mid-nineties reports appeared to have the air of correcting misapprehensions, frequently stressing the differences between the TCu380A and the Dalkon Shield. After the safety of the TCu380A seemed to no longer be in question, the focus of the papers tended to shift in cost-effectiveness of the devices, mostly relating to their long life and high effectiveness in relation to other reversible methods of birth control; a tone which continues to this day.

The high cost-effectiveness of IUDs is such an uncontroversial consensus, it extends past national borders. For example, a 2010 analysis of three different types of IUDs in China also came to the conclusion that the TCu380A was the most cost-effective method of birth control of the three studied.[2] Considering that the conclusion drawn by this study is one that has been replicated in the research literature for about twenty years, the report would be largely unremarkable save for a particular detail—the reported 2006 average device price was 2.60RMB— approximately $0.32 USD by the 2006 conversion rate.

It's currently well-known that US healthcare expenses are the highest in the world, but the copper IUD could arguably by the most arbitrageable item of all, if there weren't such harsh penalties for bringing it across the American border. How is it possible that so many TCu380As are sold for such a low price? One explanation could be that in general, estimates for the cost of manufacturing a TCu380A place the cost per device under $0.25 USD. [3] In fact, one detailed analysis of contraceptive industry in India indicates that, "The production of IUDs is more of an assembly process... Other than the need for clean rooms, the assembly of IUDs does not require the same level of investment as hormonal products."[4] It should surprise no one to hear that production costs in India or China are much lower than in the US, but it must be pointed out that Indian IUD manufacturers import most of the raw goods from the US and Europe, so the cost of raw materials is nearly identical to US and European IUDs, as is the quality of the finished product.

The production of the TCu380A is potentially the most simplistic in the pharmaceutical industry. At this point it should be noted that it may seem counterintuitive to discuss the TCu380A —which clearly appears to be a device—in relation to pharmaceuticals, but the interaction of copper ions with the female reproductive system has earned the IUD a pharmaceutical classification. The TCu380A is a unique pharmaceutical item in that it is the only drug in the FDA Orange Book which lists copper as the active ingredient, and copper is the only active ingredient of this drug.[5] Copper is of course easy to come by—you don't need a pharmaceutical company to provide it—but it appears that in the US, Teva is the only legal provider of pharmaceutical quality, uterine-grade copper.[6]

Israeli designer Ronen Kadushin has created a "political product concept" to comment on this absurd circumstance—that IUDs are simple devices which use a fraction of the amount of copper that can be found in a penny, but are made expensive by a virtue of their utility, and rendered paradoxically scarce as a consequence of their virtue. Kadushin's creation is named "Bearina", and it is a small, hollow frame which is shaped like a bear's head, with a small space in the center to insert a coin. Purely theoretically, Bearina could be used as an IUD, with the outward-facing ears of the bear's head used to anchor the IUD in the uterus in the same way that the arms of a T-shaped device anchor it in place. A penny could be inserted into Bearina's hollow center to release copper ions and inhibit fertilization in the same way the copper on the arms and stem of a standard TCu380A IUD does. While Kadushin appears hopeful that the political product concept could someday lead to 3D printing or otherwise increased contraceptive access, he explicitly clarifies

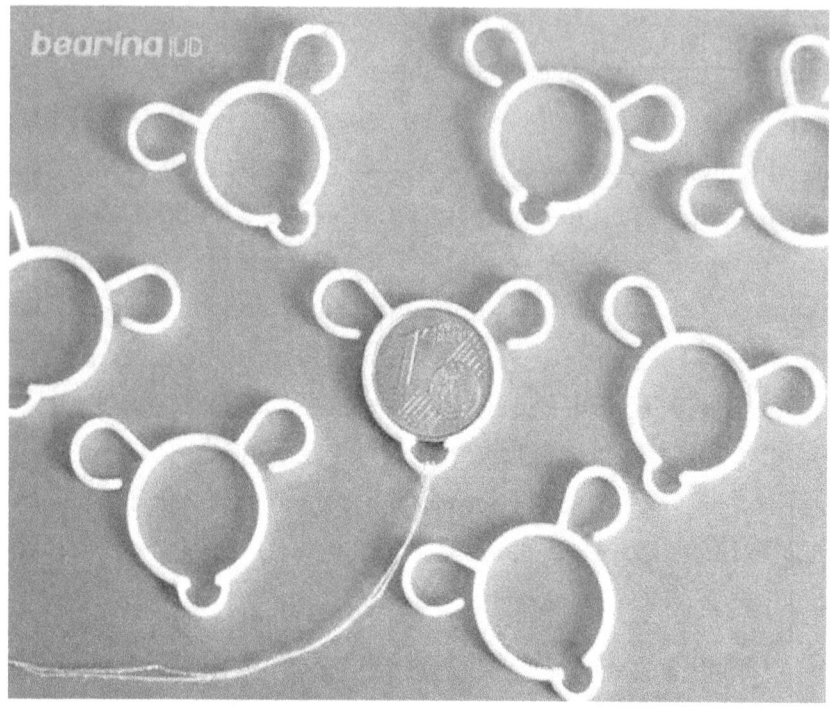

*Figure 5: The Bearina "political product concept" IUD.*
*Image courtesy of Ronen Kadushin.*

that Bearina is "concept" and not a functional IUD. Issues of hygiene aside, the increased copper content would likely make the Bearina considerably heavier than a standard copper IUD, and more likely to migrate. Additionally, the surface area of a coin is three times that of the copper in TCu380A, so unpleasant side effects would likely be increased. Needless to say, Kadushin's concept is not a comprehensive solution to the problem of prohibitively-priced IUDs. Nonetheless, the Bearina concept serves as a broader comment on the democratizing potential of 3D printing and open sourcing. The plans for Bearina can be downloaded from Kadushin's website.[7]

For the moment it does not appear that the technology of additive manufacturing is able to produce a viable IUD. For the time being, the method of manufacturing a standard TCu380A consists of:[8]

- Injection molding a T-shaped frame out of low-density polyethylene, to which barium sulfate added for X-ray opacity
- Mechanically attaching copper collars to the arms
- Mechanically winding copper filament to the stem
- Attaching a polyethylene thread to the stem, either mechanically or manually
- Sealing the device in packaging, and Gamma-ray sterilizing the unit

Because of the TCu380A's perfect combination of simplicity of design, long-term effectiveness, and economic production costs, it has been described as an, "unsung, under-promoted success story."[9]

| Global survey of copper IUD device prices, 1987-2012. All prices converted to USD at exchange rate of appropriate year | | | | |
|---|---|---|---|---|
| Year | Country | Price (as listed) | Price (PPP adjusted to USD) | Price as percent of GDP per capita |
| 1993 | USA | $109 | $109 | 0.41% |
| 1998 | Egypt | $1.46 | $3.65 | 0.04% |
| 2001 | USA | $358.80 | $358.80 | 0.96% |
| 2001 | UK | $13.16 | $14.62 | 0.04% |
| 2005 | Brazil | $3.20 | $5.33 | 0.04% |
| 2005 | Chile | $0.31 | $0.51 | 0.002% |
| 2006 | China | $0.32 | $0.80 | 0.006% |
| 2008 | Canada | $72.13 | $78.08 | 0.19% |
| 2012 | USA | $718 | $718 | 1.39% |

*Table 1. See Appendix B for details and data sources.*

The preceding chart includes a global sample of device prices for the TCu380A between 1993 and 2012, displayed as listed, compared to purchasing power parity (PPP) dollars, and compared to GDP per capita in respective year. Upon observing that many of the lowest TCu380A prices are in very low-income countries, one could easily describe differences between the US and the rest of the world as a fair reflection of the respective differences in economies or level of infrastructure. However it should be noted that if the TCu380A were priced according to the average non-US percent of GDP per capita, in 2012 it would have cost $50 instead of $718. Correspondingly, when compared to GDP per capita, European and Canadian prices are still a fraction of US prices. For example, US citizens tend to pay about twice as much than their northern neighbors for medical care,[10] but in the case of the TCu380A, US prices are ten times higher.

Further, attributing the price difference to the level of infrastructure would be highly inaccurate. For example, because of CENABAST, an autonomous procurement agency, Chile obtained the lowest TCu380A prices in all of South America, even though in the years studied they also had the highest GDP per capita. In 2005 Chile's public sector obtained IUDs for one tenth the price as in Brazil ($0.31 compared to $3.20), but Chile's GDP per capita was 50% higher than Brazil's (approximately $12,773 per capita, compared to $8,502).[11] Additionally, in the early millennial years the US GDP per capita was only three times than that of Chile, but TCu380A prices were well over one thousand times higher. It appears that, far from the costs, Chile has actually greatly enjoyed the benefits of infrastructure. Through CENABAST, Chile's procurement process has been described as, "straightforward, efficient, and transparent."[12] US medical pricing, by contrast, has been described as, "chaos behind a veil of secrecy."[13]

Charging different prices for the same product depending on where it is sold, or to whom, is called price discrimination. Despite the images the word "discrimination" conjures, price discrimination is not necessarily a bad thing and can even be a mechanism for increasing equality. Juan Rovira, Senior Health Economist of The World Bank defines prices as equitable when the price paid in each country is proportional to the average income,[14] and certainly if medical treatments were not offered on a price discriminatory basis, they would be priced out of access to people in developing nations. The point of bringing up the near-marginal (no profit) prices of copper IUDs in countries like Chile ($0.31), China ($0.32) is not to agitate for identical prices in the US, but more to give credence to the estimates that copper IUDs can be produced for under $0.25.

However, it must be observed that Rovira's definition of equity pricing may be a sufficient general starting point, but it only accounts for income inequalities between nations, and not within a country. In the 1990's Philip Harvey analyzed data from over 50 countries to develop what is now referred to as the "One Percent Rule," which describes a finding that usage rates of contraceptives universally drop if the price to the consumer is more than 1% of annual income. In 2012, even at prices close to $1,000, both the copper IUD and the LNG-IUS were not in significantly in violation of the One Percent Rule, according to US GDP per capita. [15] The reason this is problematic in the United States is that unexpected pregnancies and abortions disproportionately occur to low-income women, with 86% of unplanned births occurring to women living within 300% of the poverty line[16] and 57-69% of abortions occurring to women within 200% of the poverty line,[17] even though only half[18] and one third[19] of all American women live within those thresholds, respectively. That means that the women who were priced out of IUD access were also the women who were having nearly twice their share of unplanned births and abortions. That is to say, the women who couldn't afford the IUD are exactly the ones that needed it most.

More importantly, lack of access to reliable contraception has deep implications for issues of inequality. For example, a national survey of contraception-using women between the ages of 18-44 found that women who were concerned about costs were twice as likely as other women to rely on relatively ineffective methods of birth control, such as condoms, withdrawal, or periodic abstinence, and that one third of them would switch method if cost were not an issue.[20] That the majority of unplanned pregnancies and abortions occur among low-income women creates a circumstance in which family planning becomes a luxury of the rich, and unplanned births and abortions an intrinsic hazard of poverty. Further, there is a close relationship between the ability for a woman to control her reproductive cycles and attain educational or professional goals.[21] Allowing a circumstance in which reliable contraception is reserved for the wealthier among the population perpetuates a cycle of institutionalized classism and sexism, both of which are completely anathema to the American ideal of equality of opportunity.

To be fair, both Teva and Bayer have financial assistance programs in place. Teva offers a ParaGard® payment plan in which uninsured women can opt for eleven monthly payments of $68, or three monthly payments of $372, after the initial payment of $184 or $186.[22] And both Teva and Bayer have mechanisms in place to donate units to women if they can demonstrate poverty status, and prove that they have no insurance, nor do they qualify for Medicaid, and provided that they can find a willing healthcare practitioner to assist them—which may be difficult, considering that The Bayer-funded Arch Foundation notifies healthcare practitioners that, "Because of the current demand for the units available through the ARCH Foundation, the Foundation must limit the number of Mirena® units provided to your facility's clients to 60 units per year."[23] That is, so many poor women are in need of IUDs that Bayer must limit the number of poor women that can be given IUDs.

In the 1980's a copper IUD could be purchased for approximately $25—or $50 when adjusted for inflation and converted to 2013 dollars. By 2012 the price of a copper IUD in America had shot up to over $700, rendering the cost of the device alone (not including insertion or office visit fees), unaffordable to approximately 66% percent of American households in 2012.[24] If the One Percent Rule were used to guide IUD prices, but set based on the population with the greatest need instead of GDP per capita, it would place cost around $100. This price would still be well above that in most places of the world, but would allow quality contraceptives to be widely accessible in the United States. There is something deeply dysfunctional about a system in which a healthcare item can be produced for approximately 25 cents, sold outside of the US for under a dollar, but is unaffordable to the majority of American households.

Of course, all of this talk about who can and can't afford which contraceptives has been made irrelevant by the ACA contraceptive mandate, hasn't it? Now every woman can finally have the contraceptives she needs. But the problem of overpriced contraceptives is not going away, only going somewhere else. It may be true that within the coming years women's reproductive choices may finally represent their preferences, instead of financial situation, and incidences of unplanned pregnancy may come to be less economically stratified. The contraceptive mandate stands to improve the lives of American women considerably, and make big strides towards equality of opportunity. But it's important to remember that despite appearances, insurance coverage doesn't make things free, it just lowers the cost for an individual by distributing it among more people. The contraceptive mandate does not change the fact that monopolistic suppliers are charging Americans a hundred thousand percent markup for a very useful but very cheaply made healthcare product-except now all Americans are paying for it instead of just those who could afford it. Indeed, within America's unique context of pharmaceutical price-gauging and healthcare rationing, this may rightly be lauded as progress towards improved social welfare. But as we shall see, whether it truly represents savings or a swindle depends entirely on how the circumstances are analyzed.

# NOTES

[1]     Quoted in National Family Planning & Reproductive Health Association. "Securing Affordable Contraceptive Drugs and Devices for Title X Providers". Policy Brief. Fall 2010.

[2]     Wen (2010)

[3]     See Maurice (2002) and Beer (2006). Maurice indicated that a copper IUD costs 22 cents to produce, and Beer indicated that it cost under 25 cents. I have never seen any cost estimates that specifically pertain to the manufacture of the ParaGard® brand TCu380A, but it's reasonable to assume that the price is similar, both because the ParaGard® is not significantly different from other brands of TCu380A, and because the TCu380As made in India are made of imported mat erials, implying that the materials are the same. Further, the ParaGard®is made by Teva Pharmaceuticals, which operates in over 60 countries worldwide. Economy of scale would indicate that ParaGard® could potentially be manufactured for a lower cost than of the brands that experience more limited distribution, but for the sake of simplicity and consistency, I use 25 cents as a general estimate for the manufacturing cost of a TCu380A.

[4]     Beer (2006) Executive Summary and pg 6

[5]     The FDA Orange Book Active Ingredient Search can be found here: http://www.accessdata.fda.gov/scripts/cder/ob/docs/queryai.cfm

[6]     There is no such thing as uterine-grade copper. While some IUD manufacturers will blend their copper with silver or gold, a standard TCu380A contains oxygen-free electronic (OFE) 99.99% pure copper. This probably can't be found at the local standard hardware store, but can be purchased from any industrial metal supplier. For more details, see WHO (2010)

[7]     Bearina IUD Concept can be accessed from: http://www.ronen-kadushin.com/index.php/open-design/bearina-iud-concept/

[8]     WHO (2010)

[9]     Maurice (2002)

[10]    Reinhardt (2004) notes that in 2001 Canada spent 57% of America's per capita spending on healthcare, and the OECD average was 44%. Considering the current focus on healthcare in the US, this report was quite prescient in remarking that, "while these trends are not an imminent burden on the macro economy, they will place an increasing burden on the members of lower-income groups even within the coming decade."

[11]    GDP per capita data obtained from the World Bank: http://data.worldbank.org/indicator/NY.GDP.PCAP.PP.CD

[12]    Sarley (2006) pg 11

[13]     Reinhardt (2006). To be fair, Reinhardt was describing hospital pricing, but his words perfectly describe my search for verifiable pharmaceutical prices as well.

[14]     Rovira, (2003)

[15]     At the 2012 price of $718, the price of the ParaGard® IUD is only 1.3% of the GDP per capita of the United States in 2012, and the cost of a Mirena® device is only 1.6%.

[16]     Mosher (2012) pg 13 reports that 14% of unintended births occur to women that live above 300% of the poverty line, with the remaining 86% of unintended births are to women below. This data refers to births happening between 2001 and 2006.

[17]     Jones (2010) pg 6 reports that in 2000 57% of abortions were performed on women living within 200% of the poverty line, and that number jumped to 69% in 2008.

[18]     The US Census reports that 50.4% of women lived below 300% of the poverty line in 2005. Data can be accessed: http://www.census.gov/hhes/www/cpstables/macro/032006/pov/new01_300_01.htm

[19]     The US Census reports that 34.1% of women lived below 200% of the poverty line in 2008. Data can be accessed: http://www.census.gov/hhes/www/cpstables/032009/pov/new01_200_01.htm

[20]     Frost (2008b)

[21]     See Brown (1995), Frost (2012), Guttmacher (2013b), and Klima (1998) among others.

[22]     When this book was initially written in 2014, the ParaGard®official website offered payment plans of

nineteen monthly payments of $39, twelve monthly payments of $62, or three monthly payments of $151, after the initial payment of $299. By January 31st 2014 it had changed to the plans described in the text. Acces sible: http://www.paragard.com/What-it-costs.aspx

[23]    Arch Foundation website, accessible:

http://www.archfoundation.com/providers.htm

[24]    DeNavas-Walt (2013) pg 33 indicates that in 2012 13% of Americans had an income of under $15,000 a year, 11.7% between $15,000 and $24,999, 10.7% between $25,000 and $34,999, 13.6% between $35,000 and $49,999, and 17.5% between $50,000 and $74,9999, to a total of 66.5% under $75,000.

# CHAPTER 4

## IN AN IUDEAL WORLD

*"High costs and failure to achieve value for money in our health system are not merely economic failings. They are also ethical problems. If we have a health system that delivers health services at very high cost per unit of benefit delivered— and the US system has the highest unit costs in the world— then we can meet fewer health needs than a more efficient system would."*

Daniels, et al. Access, Cost, And Financing: Achieving An Ethical Health Reform. 2009

*"While some companies attempt to develop value-added features, IUDs have become a commodity, that is, the product and quality are uniform throughout the industry—a point manufacturers acknowledge."*

Beer, et al. Assessment of India's locally manufactured contraceptive product supply. 2006.

Unplanned births cost US taxpayers between $9.6 and $12 billion dollars per year. Nearly half of all births in the US are paid for by Medcaid, with a higher percentage for unintended births. [1] Nearly half of all unintended pregnancies happen to women who are already using birth control,[2] which is unsurprising considering that most contracepting women use methods with a relatively high failure rate, such as condoms or the birth control pill. Of the women who did not use contraception prior to an unintended birth between 2006 and 2008, 35% indicated that the reason they were not using birth control because they did not think that they could get pregnant.[3] That there are so many women who are both reproductively-aged and sexually active, but do not think that they can get pregnant, indicates that the US has an urgent need to increase awareness of the consequences of unprotected sex and increase easy access to birth control. However, even if the US were to solely focus on the women who are already using birth control, and help them make more effective contraceptive choices, billions of dollars per year could be saved in taxpayer funds.

Multiple studies have reported that money invested in public birth control leads to savings in public funds. Recent findings include:

- In 2001 unplanned pregnancies cost US taxpayers between, $9.6 billion and $12.6 billion.[4] Researchers claimed that preventing unintended pregnancies would save between $4.7 billion and $6.2 billion. The estimate of the average taxpayer cost per publicly subsidized unintended pregnancy was $9,000.

- In 2003 California's PACT (Planning Access Care and Treatment) program saved $3.52 for every $1 spent on family planning.[5] Even at a total cost of over $400 per device and doctor visit fees, IUDs saved $7.24 for every $1 that went towards their procurement and distribution.

- In 2004, the $1.4 billion spent on family planning averted an estimated 1.4 million pregnancies, 641 thousand births, and 602 thousand abortions among the 6.9 million women served.[6] The prevention of these events saved taxpayers an estimated $5.7 billion that would have otherwise been spent on unintended births. Researchers concluded that for every $1 that is spent on publicly funded family planning, $4.02 is saved.

- An analysis of the data from the Pregnancy Risk Assessment Monitoring System found that $11.1 billion was spent on unplanned births in 2006.[7] This represents half of all public money spent on births.

- An analysis of hospital records, looking at pregnancy costs and probability of repeat pregnancy from 2002 to 2006, reported that the state government would save $2.94 for every dollar spent on a state-financed IUD program.[8]

- In 2013 Trussell et al. estimated that the cost savings of long-acting reversible contraception were such that if even 10% of women aged 20–29 years switched from oral contraception to LARC, total costs would be reduced by $288 million per year.

Though each of the aforementioned studies utilized different methods to estimate savings from prevented events, the results tend to be fairly consistent across studies. Foster et al. used arguably the most sophisticated—and laborious—technique, looking at the records of women who accessed California's Planning Access Care and Treatment (PACT) services and predicting rates of pregnancy based on failure rates for the prior birth control method. For example, if a woman had used condoms as a primary birth control method prior to obtaining oral contraceptives from PACT, Foster et al. predicted the likelihood of an unplanned pregnancy for her based on condom failure rates. The aggregate number of expected pregnancies based on failure rates for prior birth control methods was then compared to expected pregnancies compared to failure rates of current contraceptives obtained under PACT, to estimate averted events. Foster et al.'s data indicate that on average, PACT family planning assistance prevented 257 unplanned pregnancies per 1,000 users, with varying rates depending on effectiveness of contraceptive method. For example, IUDs prevented 500 unplanned pregnancies per 1,000 users, compared to 201 unplanned pregnancies per 1,000 pill users, or 40 unplanned pregnancies per 1,000 barrier method users.[9]

Using different methodology Frost et al. reported similar findings, estimating that publicly funded family planning across the country prevented an average 242 pregnancies per 1,000 users. From that estimate Frost et al. reported that publicly funded family planning prevented 108 unplanned births per 1,000 users, and 101 abortions, for a total of 1.4 million unplanned pregnancies, 641 thousand unplanned births, and 602 thousand abortions prevented per year. In short: no matter how the data analyzed, it's clear that public money is more efficiently spent on preventative family planning than on the unplanned births that occur in its absence.

A close study of cost-effectiveness research in contraception over the past twenty years reveals the apparent limits of the American academic imagination. Researchers regularly estimate the cost of unplanned pregnancy based on real numbers of pregnancies, births, and abortions in the United States and average prices for medical care. Researchers use models to make projections of hypothetical pregnancies, births, and abortions that never happened (but might have in absence of services) and estimate the savings accrued from money spent on family planning services. Researches frequently cite high upfront cost as a lamentable barrier to IUD usage, and stress the importance ignoring the cost in the interest of public health. But seldom do any researchers try to imagine a world in which IUDs were more affordable, and never do they question why a sterilized piece of plastic and copper should cost nearly a thousand dollars. The unspoken implication is that it's more credible to imagine a medically regressive dystopia in which women have little control over their reproductive cycles than it is to imagine a world in which the United States has control over pharmaceutical prices.

This pertinent absence in the collective national imagination has given birth to a peculiar rationalization that as long as the price of the IUD remains well under that of an unplanned birth or abortion, it remains a bargain, regardless of the annual inflation or largess of price markup. For example, as noted in the introduction of this volume, one analysis of in-hospital IUD insertions for the purpose of preventing repeat unplanned pregnancies claimed a cost-effectiveness price ceiling of IUDs that was in excess of ten thousand dollars per device![10] An issue which needs to be discussed is the perversity of circumstances in which the price of a sterilized piece of plastic and copper can skyrocket indefinitely and yet continue to avoid public scrutiny. Some might say that it would be inappropriate for a reproductive researcher to comment on the price of medical products, and that the role of the researcher is only to evaluate safety and effectiveness. It may be true that price comparisons threaten to turn academia into advertisements, but the fact of the matter is that researchers have already been commenting on the cost-effectiveness of various contraceptive methods for decades—at times with clear industry funding.[11] Academic inquiry has been demoted to engaging in product price comparisons for decades, but so far only a very limited set of options have been explored. It's time to move past the issue of cost-effectiveness and begin to discuss the effect of the cost.

Possibly the best estimate of the effect cost has on IUD usage comes from the Contraceptive CHOICE Project,[12] which found that, if educated about all and given her choice of contraceptives free of charge, 67% of contraceptive-seeking women will choose a long-acting method, and 56% will choose an IUD. That this number is ten times higher than the 5.5% IUD usage rate reported by the most recent National Survey of Family Growth (NSFG) implies that cost is a highly prohibiting factor in IUD usage. The researchers concluded that removing financial barriers to methods of long acting contraception would increase use, but they did not stipulate exactly how these barriers would be removed. Nonetheless, The Contraceptive CHOICE project has provided a valuable response to over a decade's worth of researchers asking why IUDs are so under-utilized in the United States. To paraphrase Gerard Anderson's famous explanation cutting to the heart of why healthcare in the US costs more than it does in any other country: "It's the prices, stupid."[13]

This implication is strengthened by a 2002 study which found that after Kaiser Permanente Northern California eliminated cost-sharing from IUDs, implants, and injectable, IUD use increased by 137%.[14] Additionally, in 2011 researchers analyzed records from a family planning clinic and found that IUD prices could reach as high as $800, but women were five times more likely to obtain an IUD when the out-of-pocket cost was under $50.[15]

When one considers that the US price of the TCu380A has been well over $50 for the past twenty years, it begins to appear quite obvious why the US has the lowest IUD usage rates of any developed nation[16]—and rates of unplanned[17] and teen[18] pregnancies significantly higher than in other developed nations.

Frost et al. estimated that over two hundred thousand women in 2002 both used publicly funded contraceptive services, and used IUDs.[19] One can safely assume these IUDs were provided with public funds, because a woman who can afford the upfront costs of an IUD has no need for publicly funded contraceptive services —a woman who already has an IUD in place has little need for contraceptive services at all. This estimate—that two hundred thousand of the eight hundred thousand total American IUD users in 2002 utilized public family planning services—is consistent with a random sample survey of women in California between the years of 1997 and 2007, which found the approximately 20% of sampled IUD users had received their device through publicly funded entities.[20]

Price instability and secrecy in the US medical industry makes it impossible to precisely estimate how many tax dollars have gone towards IUD public procurement. Medical pricing is notoriously secretive, to the degree that even medical professionals may find themselves unable to find and compare prices for medical commodities. Nonetheless, because researchers have been commenting on the cost-effectiveness of various contraceptives for decades, some form of pricing data can be mottled together. For example, one paper cites the 1993 device price to the public sector as $109. [21] Another paper indicated in 2002 the price was $164,[22] and Foster estimated the price in 2003 around $400, but that price includes both device price and doctors visit fees. Taken together these three papers imply that the public sector price of the TCu380A was fairly stable for many years, and that paradoxically, the public sector price of a ParaGard® IUD did not really start to skyrocket until after it faced monopolistic competition from Mirena® in the early millennial years.

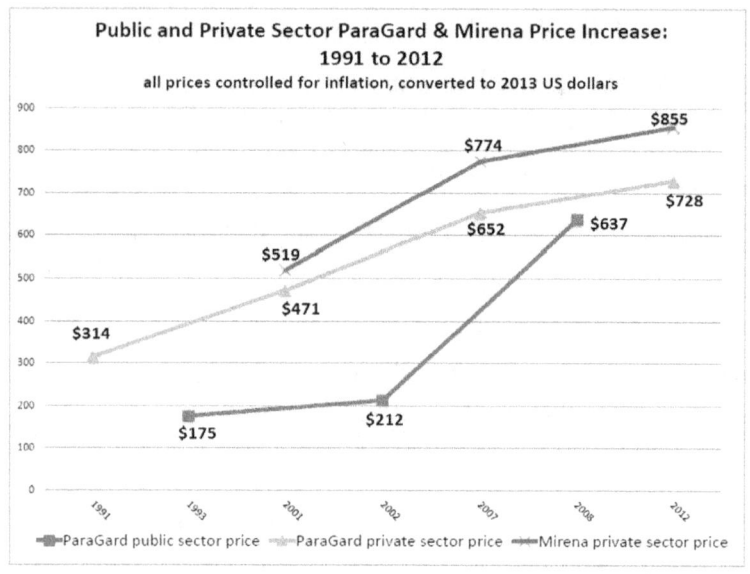

**Public and Private Sector ParaGard & Mirena Price Increase: 1991 to 2012**
all prices controlled for inflation, converted to 2013 US dollars

*Figure 6: See Appendix C for data and sources.*

If we average the two more precise public sector values to get an admittedly rough estimate of $136 between the years of 1993 and 2002 (intentionally neglecting to control for inflation), it appears that US taxpayers had to have paid at least $37.6 million dollars[23] to provide two hundred thousand IUDs to Frost et al.'s 2002 users. In all likelihood the total expenditure would have been considerably higher to account for women who received an IUD and discontinued use prior to the 2002, but in order to err on the side of underestimating costs to the public purse, that factor will be ignored.

It's deceptively simplifying to put too much faith in thought experiments, but they can nonetheless be somewhat illustrative of potential alternatives. Instead of using hypothetical effects of contraceptives to justify increased public expenditures on grossly marked-up medical devices, I have imagined an IUDeal World in which, rather than paying record-high pharmaceutical prices, the US was able to leverage its market strength to procure TCu380As for prices similar to those enjoyed in other countries around a similar time period. Calculating the number of IUDs that could have been purchased for the same amount of public funds that were already spent on overpriced IUDs gives a microcosmic view of how much money is unnecessarily wasted on exorbitant pharmaceutical pricing in the US.

| Global public sector copper IUD prices, circa 2001-2005 | | Estimated total public funds spent on IUDs prior to 2002 | Number copper IUDs purchasable for allotted expenditure |
|---|---|---|---|
| US | $136 USD | | .2 million |
| UK | $13.16 USD | $37.6 million | 2.8 million |
| Brazil | $3.20 USD | | 11.7 million |
| Chile | $0.31 USD | | 121.4 million |

*Table 2. See text, Appendix B for details and data sources.*

The potential amount of IUDs at the Chilean price is offered as a point of comparison—in any given year there are only 60 million women of reproductive age in the US, and only about 38 million using any form of contraception at all. 121 million more than triples the number of contraceptive-using women in the entire United States, let alone the number that might be interested in using an IUD. The point is only to illustrate that for the same amount of money that was spent providing contraceptives to approximately 0.44% of reproductively-aged women in America, safe and reliable long-acting contraceptives could have been purchased in quantities that greatly exceed the needs of the entire population of contraceptive users, and doubles the number of reproductively-aged women total. When the price of IUDs in America are compared to prices in other countries, rather than the standard comparison to the also overpriced cost of a birth in America,[24] they begin to look considerably less cost-effective and considerably more cost-extravagant.

In 2002 there were an estimated 16.7 million women in need of publicly funded contraceptive services.[25] If IUDs were available in the US at near-marginal prices, as they are in Chile or China, sufficient IUDs could have been provided for that entire reproductively-aged female population for only $5.2 million, with an additional $32.4 million to spare from the $37.6 million IUD allotment amount. This stands in stark contrast to the real world of exorbitantly-priced IUDs, in which over eight times as much money went to provide contraceptives to less than half of one percent of the reproductively-aged American population.

Of course, not every American woman is interested in family planning, and not every contracepting woman is interested in an IUD. The fact that between 20-30% discontinue use of their IUD after the first year[26] indicates that for some, the unpleasant side effects outweigh the benefits. It's important to note that even after only one year the 70-80% continuation rate IUDs experience is considerably higher than the 55% continuation rate of short acting contraceptives such as condoms, but it would nonetheless be unreasonable to expect copper IUDs to be a perfect solution for everyone.

To estimate the maximum potential of American women that might want an IUD, we can look to the Contraceptive CHOICES

Project, which found that 56% of contraceptive seeking women would choose an IUD if cost were not an issue. The CHOICES results are not perfectly suited for the IUDeal World thought experiment, because CHOICES examined the usage rates if all contraceptive options were free of charge, so it's not clear if, for example, the 5:1 preference that women revealed for hormonal IUDs over copper IUDs would be nullified if copper IUDs were free and hormonal IUDs—or implants, or injectable, or various other contraceptive options—were not. In posing this question I should not be misconstrued as to be encouraging public health providers to limit their options solely to copper IUDs. However, due to the fact that copper IUDs can be economically mass produced and stored for up to 5 years with no harm to the device's safety and effectiveness, they are a clear favorite for public bulk procurement.[27] For the purposes of the IUDeal World thought experiment we will use 56% as a maximum percentage of contracepting women within a population who might choose an IUD if offered free of charge, but the imperfection of this estimation is readily acknowledged. More research is clearly needed to evaluate how cost prohibits usage rates specifically in the copper IUD.

If 56% of the 16 million American women who were in need of publicly funded family planning services had used IUDs in 2002, that would have constituted 9.3 million users. According to Foster et al.'s method of estimating unplanned pregnancy preventions, providing for an additional 9.3 million IUD users would have resulted in a reduction of 2.4 million unplanned pregnancies per year. A reduction of 2.4 million unplanned pregnancies could mean approximately 1.1 million fewer unplanned births, and potentially between 8 hundred thousand to 1 million abortions prevented *in a single year*.[28]

Insertion and doctor visit fees for IUDs in the public sector ranged from somewhat under to slightly over $100.[29] Factoring in a hypothetical fixed $100 IUD doctor's fee, providing IUDs to an additional 9.1 million users would require an additional $910 million dollars. However, a 1.1 million reduction in unplanned births would result in savings of approximately 9.9 billion dollars, to a net savings of nearly 9 billion dollars in a single year. Addition savings would continue to accrue in subsequent years as the majority of IUD users continued use of their device with no additional cost to public funds. Recall that this reduction in unplanned pregnancies is based on 9.1 million additional IUD users, when in fact the number of IUDs that could have been purchased at marginal prices is well over 9.1 million.

| | Women receiving public services | Unplanned pregnancies | Births resulting from unplanned pregnancies | Abortions | Effect on public funds |
|---|---|---|---|---|---|
| Real World annualized events and public expenditures[30] | | | | | |
| Real World 2001-2002 | 6.9 million | 3.1 million occurred | 1.5 million occurred | 1.2 million occurred | $9.6-$12.6 billion expenditures |
| Annual potential savings and preventions based on lower price and increased IUD usage | | | | | |
| IUDeal World | 16 million | 2.4 million prevented | 1.1 million prevented | 0.8-1 million prevented | $9 billion net savings |

*Table 3. Most data cited in text. Details and sources in Appendix A*

It could be said that this return on an investment is true for all reliable contraceptives, and in a purely numerical sense that is true. The $9 billion savings in the IUDeal World is primarily related to increased usage of highly reliable, long acting methods of contraception, not necessarily the cost of device procurement. On the other end of the pricing spectrum, even at $400 per device and doctor fees, Foster et al. found that IUDs incurred savings seven times higher than the costs of procurement and distribution. In short: preventative contraception is cost-effective at nearly any price.

However, something that needs to be considered is the effect the high cost of IUDs has had on reducing client access. For example, in 2010 the CDC conducted a mailed survey on contraceptive provision, and found that 40% of the 2,000 Title X clinics sampled did not even have copper IUDs on site.[31] The Dalkon scare has been over for decades, and long-acting methods of contraception are now universally accepted as the best method for preventing unintended pregnancy, and yet copper IUDs are unavailable in nearly half of the Title X clinics—exactly where they would be needed in order to prevent 86% of all unintended births. The CDC findings were further echoed by the 2010 policy brief for the National Family Planning and Reproductive Health Association: "The bottom line for Title X providers, however, is that the high cost of contraceptive drugs and devices prevent some health centers from being able to provide the fullest range of effective methods, to the detriment of the patient."[32] Another researcher further notes that the high cost of devices puts providers in a catch-22: "To negotiate a deep discount, it would need to demonstrate substantial demand among its members, something it cannot do at current prices."[33]

Medically, an expensive IUD can prevent unintended births just as well as a marginally-priced one can. The uterus does not price discriminate. But only by reducing the cost of IUDs can we ensure that they will be sufficiently accessible to have the maximum impact on unintended pregnancies. It's been said that with medical pricing, you get the care you pay for—that is, consumers who are willing to pay more get better access. But in the United

States, where 65% of births are covered by Medicaid, everyone pays when women can't afford effective contraceptives. Pricing reliable contraception with the priority of maximizing access rather than profits would result in money being diverted more efficiently, instead of rewarding excessive pharmaceutical profit-seeking. In the case of contraceptive insecurity and Medicaid expenditures on unplanned births, allowing the price of IUDs to climb sufficiently to cause relative scarcity costs the taxpayers 9 billion dollars a year.

Further, for over a decade the issue of abortion has been framed in a national debate of life vs. choice. Advocates have become so consumed by the conflict they've failed to observe the false dichotomy in which they've become mired. Contraceptive access before conception—or even up to 5 days after intercourse, in the case of the TCu380A—can give women a choice without entering the moral quagmire of whether or not she is ending a life. This common-sense notion is confirmed in the research literature. For example, an analysis of trends in Asia and Europe noted that as access to modern birth control methods increased rapidly in the 1990s, abortion rates declined significantly,[34] with a strong, clear, and negative correlation between contraceptive use within a country and abortion rates per woman. That is to say, as use in contraceptives increased, abortions radically decreased.

Similarly, in the Republic of Georgia—a country with an unfortunately high lifetime average of 3.7 abortions per woman—an increase in contraceptive use accounted for 54% of a subsequent decline in abortion rates.[35] In the United States the Contraceptive CHOICE project found that the women in their sample who were given free contraceptives experienced abortion rates that were between one fourth to one half the national rate in years observed, leading researchers to conclude that if the US policy were to distribute contraceptives as freely as did CHOICE, between 62-78% of abortions performed annually in the United States would be prevented.[36] In realistic terms, that means that universal access to reliable contraceptives could prevent nearly *one million abortions* in just one year.

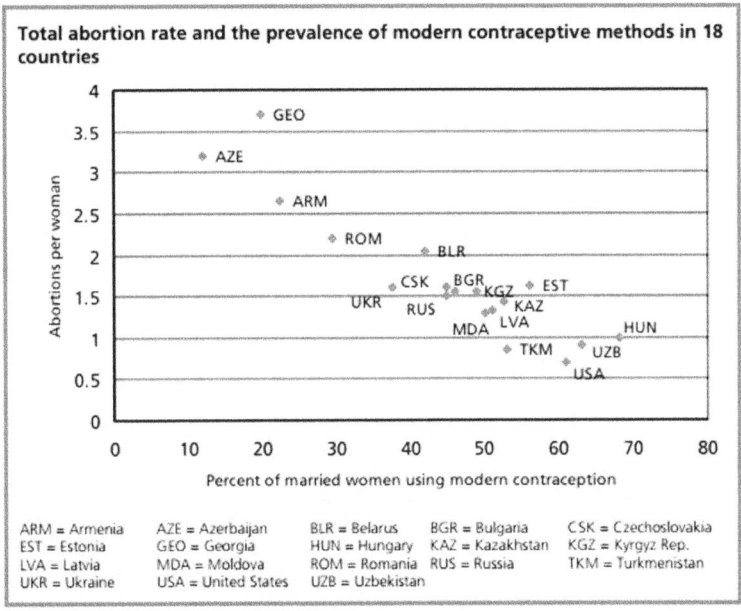

*Figure 7: Source: Westoff (2005)*

Materials and technology exist such that reliable contraception could be cheaply distributed to effectively make abortion an uncommon event; a relic of a Hobbesian past. Instead, over 1.2 million abortions are performed in the United States per year, to an average of over 3,000 abortions per day. Rather than pointing fingers at individual pregnancies and abortion providers, it's time for Americans to stand back and see the larger picture. Americans must now critically analyze the institutional mechanism which have unnecessarily perpetuated obstacles to American contraceptive security and affordable health care access.

# NOTES

[1]    Mosher (2012) pg 24 reports that of all births occurring between 2001 and 2006, 46.1% were paid for with Medicaid—approximately 9.7 million of the 21 million total births. 35.2% (4.6 million) of intended births were paid for with Medicaid, as were 64.6% (5 million) of unintended births.

[2]    Mosher (2012) pg 9 reports that 40% of all unintended births occur to women who were using contraception at the time. This estimate does not include unintended pregnancies that become induced abortions.

[3]    In two Mosher reports from the National Survey of Family Growth estimates range from 35.9% to 43.9% of unintended births resulting from the mother not believing that she could get pregnant. Mosher (2010) pg 22 and Mosher (2012) pg 22.

[4]    Monea (2011)

[5]    Foster (2009)

[6]    Frost et al., (2008)

[7]    Sonfield (2011)

[8]    Rodriguez (2010)

[9]    Foster (2009) does not specify pregnancies averted per

user per method. The report indicates how many pregnancies were averted per method, and how many women used each method. I used that data to extract pregnancies prevented per method user.

[10]     Rodriguez (2010)

[11]     It should be noted that the most recent 2013 Trussell et al. paper includes the following disclosure:

"Anna Filonenko is a full-time employee of Bayer Pharma AG. Amy Law and Alexander Prezioso are full-time employees of Bayer Healthcare Pharmaceuticals Inc. Nathaniel Henry and Fareen Hassan are full-time employees of IMS Health and served as paid consultants to Bayer Healthcare Pharmaceuticals Inc. for the development of this study and manuscript. James Trussell is a full-time professor of economics and public affairs at Princeton University and received a consultancy fee from Bayer Pharma AG fort his contribution to this work."

Every single contributor to this paper has financial ties to Bayer Pharmaceuticals, one of the two sole companies approved to supply IUDs to the American public. The authors' financial ties to Bayer help explain two curious aspects of this paper related to IUD pricing. First, the price of an IUD (ParaGard®) and IUS (Mirena®) are listed as $598 and $703, which stands in stark contrast to a letter to the editor—also written by James Trussell—in the same journal only two issues prior, in which the prices of IUDs and IUSs are reported to be $718 and

$844. Both sets of prices refer to 2012, so it's unclear why there is over $120-$144 difference between the two sets for the same medication in the same year. The most obvious difference between the two papers is that the letter to the editor was not funded by Bayer Pharmaceuticals and presumably less biased. If nothing else this difference shows how wildly drug prices vary, if there can be such a discrepancy even in papers written by the same author in the same year.

It's additionally noteworthy that when averaging the cost-effectiveness of IUDs in this paper, the cost was divided by the maximum life of the device; 5 years for Mirena® and 10 years for ParaGard®. This approach is at the very least questionable, because it is well known that the majority of users do not retain their IUDs for the maximum life of the device. A more honest approach would have divided the device cost by average years of use. For example, when Rodriguez et al. (2010) incorporated real expulsion and discontinuation rates into their cost analysis they predicted that after 1 year 80.3% of women in a state-funded IUD program would continue use. Rodriguez predicted 70.9%, 64%, and 59.3% continuation in the 2nd, 3rd, and 4th years after the initial placement. Kaneshiro (2010) reports that approximately 50% of IUD users discontinue after 5 years and only approximately 28-40% continue to use an IUD for 10 years. To annualize the device price in the way Trussell et al. did, based on maximum potential years of use instead of average years of actual use is another slight bias that can serve to make the devices appear less expensive and more cost-effective than they actually are.

That's not to say that a price-bias disqualifies the entire paper. James Trussell has been writing about the cost-effectiveness of long-acting birth control for over 20 years. It's likely that Bayer approached him because he has become an authority on the subject, and the financial interest was not the cause but rather a consequence of the direction of his research. Further, the conclusions of this paper are consistent with a wide body of evidence that increased use of reliable contraceptives would result in decrease in unplanned pregnancy, births, and abortions. The biases in this paper just serve as an example of the ways funding can affect research methodology, and stresses the importance of moving past the paper abstract to read all of the fine print, especially in industry-funded research.

[12]    Secura (2010)

[13]    Anderson (2003)

[14]    Postlethwaite (2007). The study also noted a decrease in pregnancies related to contraceptive failure, unsurprisingly.

[15]    Gariepy (2011)

[16]    Hubacher 2002

[17]    Guttmacher Institute, Facts on unintended pregnancy in the United States, In Brief, 2013a.

[18]    Flynn (2013)

[19]    Frost estimates that 4% of 6.923 publicly funded family planning users relied on IUDs, which gives us

approximately 276,920 women.

[20]     Thompson (2011)

[21]     Trussell et al. (1995, 1997a)

[22]     Rodriguez (2010)

[23]     276,920 users at $136 per device is $37,661,120.

[24]     A New York Times article written by Elizabeth Rosen thal reports that a person whose insurance did not cover maternity care, "called her local hospital inquiring about the price of maternity care; the finance office at first said it did not know, and then gave her a range of $4,000 to $45,000." Rosenthal quotes a report that, "The average total price charged for pregnancy and newborn care was about $30,000 for a vaginal delivery and $50,000 for a C-section, with commercial insurers paying out an average of $18,329 and $27,866." In other countries prices were closer to $2,000 to $5,000.

[25]     Frost (2010) pg 12 reports 16,776,730 in need of publicly funded contraceptive services, as defined by a woman who is sexually active without trying to get pregnant and either under the age of 18, or at least 19 and living within 250% of the federal poverty line.

[26]     Piepert (2001) reports that in a study of 4,167 women aged 14-45, the 12 month continuation rate for ParaGard® and Mirena® was 80% and 85%, respectively. The continuation rate was lower for adolescents than for adults, at 72%. By contrast, the continuation rate for short-acting contraception was only 55%. Additionally, Hatcher (2007) reports that 78% of

women will continue to use the Copper T-380A after a year compared with 68% of women who were given oral contraceptive pills and 56% of women who received injectable contraception. These results are echoed by a study of women from developing nations (368 women from Brazil, Guatemala, Vietnam and Egypt) and randomized to receive either a copper IUD or Depot Medroxy Progesterone Acetate (DMPA) shot (Feldblum et al., 2005). After 12 months 77% of women were still using the IUD, compared to 58% of women using DMPA. The similarity of results between studies across very different nations with different levels of development and economies suggest that these results are highly generalizable.

[27]    WHO (2010)

[28]    To get this estimate I estimated the maximum amount of potential IUD users (56% of contraceptors) taken from Secura (2010) from the 16,776,730 women in need reported by Frost (2010) yields an estimate of 9,394,968 American IUD users in 2002. Less the 276,920 women who really did receive an IUD in 2002 Real World yields 9,118,048 additional IUDeal World IUD users.

Next I averaged pregnancy prevention rates extracted from Foster (2009). On average, contraceptive use averted 257 pregnancies per thousand users, with a non-IUD prevention average of 230 per thousand. The IUD specific prevention rate was 500 per thousand, so I considered the difference (270) the preventions per thousand that would have occurred from switching to IUDs. 9,118,048 additional IUDeal World IUD users.

Next I averaged pregnancy prevention rates extracted from Foster (2009). On average, contraceptive use averted 257 pregnancies per thousand users, with a non-IUD prevention average of 230 per thousand. The IUD specific prevention rate was 500 per thousand, so I considered the difference (270) the preventions per thousand that would have occurred from switching to IUDs. 9,118,048 additional IUD users could prevent 2,461,872 unplanned pregnancies.

Frost (2010) estimates that 44.6% of unintended pregnancies result in birth and 41.7% result in abortion, with the remaining 13.6% leading to fetal losses. Trussell (2012) estimated that 46.3% of all unplanned pregnancies become live births and 35.6% become induced abortions, with the remaining 18.1% spontaneous abortions and ectopic pregnancies. Borrowing Foster's estimation method with Frost's and Trussell's birth and abortion statistics yielded the IUDeal World estimates.

Applying Frost's and Trussell's estimates of births and abortions from unplanned pregnancies yields estimates that 9,118,048 additional IUD users could prevent 2,461,872 unplanned pregnancies, between 1,097,994 and 1,139,846 unplanned births, and between 876,426 and 1,026,601 abortions.

[29]    Rodriguez (2010) cites the 2002 insertion price at $106. Trussell (1995) lists a 1993 insertion price as $62.42, which is $77 in 2002 dollars. Chiou (2003) lists a 2000

insertion fee of $97.01.

[30]    Based on available data and estimates for 2001 and 2002. Estimate of 6.9 million women receiving public services taken from Frost (2010). Unplanned pregnancy estimate of 3.1 million taken from Trussell (2012). Estimate of 1.4 million unplanned births taken from CDC National Survey of Family Growth (Mosher 2012, pg 17) and annualized. Figure of 1.2 million abortions taken from CDC vital statistics (Ventura, 2012) pg 9. Public funding expenditure taken from Monea (2011).

[31]    Moskosky (2011)

[32]    National Family Planning & Reproductive Health Association. "Securing Affordable Contraceptive Drugs and Devices for Title X Providers". Policy Brief. Fall 2010.

[33]    Sonfield (2011a)

[34]    Westoff (2005)

[35]    Serbanescu (2010)

[36]    Piepert (2012)

# PART II:

## AMERICAN MEDICINE CORRUPTED

*"The fact that there is asymmetric information in the drug market, and often third party payers, adds hugely to the inefficiency. The existence of asymmetric information, where the drug company will generally know more about its product than doctors, and much more than patients, creates a situation in which companies stand to make huge profits by making misleading or even false claims about their drugs. There are numerous well-documented instances in which drug companies have withheld research findings from the public or even misrepresented their findings. This is a predictable outcome of a situation in which firms can earn above normal profits as a result of government granted patent monopoly."*

Baker. Financing Drug Research: What are the issues? 2004.

# CHAPTER 5
## WHEN DOCTORS BECOME DRUG DEALERS

*"[T]he Food and Drug Administration has suffered much embarrassment and criticism over their 'loose standards' toward conflict of interest with the industry."*

Wei. Should prizes replace patents? ...

*"Several speakers made the point that it is currently more profitable and easier to counterfeit and adulterate medicines than to sell illicit drugs."*

Pew Charitable Trusts. After Heparin: Protecting Consumers from the Risks of Substandard and Counterfeit Drugs. 2011

I t's obvious that American women are hurt by lack of access to affordable, reliable contraception. After all, a woman who has difficulty with the upfront cost of a $932 contraceptive will have a much more difficult time covering the costs of an unintended pregnancy and childbirth. I've also demonstrated that taxpayers are also paying the high price of unaffordable

IUDs. But another group increasingly marginalized by the cost of IUDs is healthcare professionals.

Medicare and Medicaid are both forms of the public contract model, which means that a person who uses either as a form of insurance will choose a private clinic from which to receive services, and then the healthcare provider will bill Medicare or Medicaid to receive reimbursement for services rendered. This can be problematic, especially for small healthcare providers, because they are not reimbursed based on their actual costs but rather on a Medicare/Medicaid's own pricing metric. If a healthcare provider is unable to negotiate good prices for pharmaceuticals and other medical goods, they stand to lose money by providing services to Medicaid/Medicare clients if the reimbursement amount is lower than expenses to the clinic. For this reason it is not uncommon to find healthcare centers refusing to see clients unless they have private insurance. The difficulty Medicare and Medicaid clients have in finding primary care physicians to treat them has been identified as a contributing factor to overcrowding and subsequently preventable deaths in US hospital emergency rooms. [1]

Healthcare centers that choose to make a commitment to providing care regardless of a patient's income status are increasingly finding themselves in a difficult position. The National Family Reproductive Health Association 2010 policy brief has reported that, "Instability in [contraceptive] prices can be devastating to a health center's budget". Another news article stated that, "Medicaid programs across the country pay so little that many physicians turn away such patients, lest they go broke."[2] Clearly limited financial resources would necessitate dispersing expensive treatments sparingly, but some have argued that, "withholding information about the copper IUD [as emergency contraception] raises ethical concerns about quality of care."[3] An apparent inability to reconcile the opposing demands of costs and care has caused some doctors to turn towards so-called "black market IUDs."

- In 2008 Dr. Angela Cope was one of six doctors sued by the Texas Attorney General for purchasing Mirena® from Canadian pharmacies and distributing them in a Texas healthcare center. When interviewed she reported that, "Mirena is a registered trademarked product. It is produced in a single plant. That plant is in Finland. And from Finland, it is distributed worldwide...From a medical perspective, the IUD itself is exactly the same. It's a misnomer to say a Canadian IUD versus an American IUD. And you know really a Canadian uterus is not any different than an American uterus."[4] Nonetheless, her patients felt like it was a, "complete betrayal of confidence." The Texas prosecuting the case requested that Cope and her five co-workers each pay $25,000 per day per violation. Court documents from the case indicate that, "Defendants allegedly purchased lower cost Mirena® IUDs because of the increasing number of uninsured patients seen by them and the fact that they were losing money each time they provided a Mirena® IUD purchased from the authorized distributor."[5] Shortly after this case both Bayer and the FDA sent a memo to discourage American healthcare providers from purchasing "foreign products,"[6] completely ignoring the highly subjective definition of what constitutes "foreign" in a Finnish-made IUD purchased in Canada or America from a German company.

- In 2010 multiple doctors in Rhode Island, Massachusetts, and Kentucky were investigated and charged with inserting up to 400 Canadian-purchased Mirena® IUDs in their patients.[7]

- In 2011 Kelly Dean Shrum of Arkansas was sentenced to 3 years' probation and ordered to pay $204,194.49 restitution and to forfeit $75,000 of proceeds from the health care fraud after federal agents searched his office and found IUDs, "labeled in Scandinavian and Turkish languages."[8] Shrum additionally suffered a civil lawsuit in which former patients alleged that Dr. Shrum is at fault for medical negligence, unjust enrichment, violation of the state's law against deceptive trade practices, and breach of fiduciary duty. Shrum's defense claims that the IUDs were purchased legitimately to, "reduce unnecessary healthcare costs that are greatly increased by pharmaceutical companies charging Americans the highest prices in the world for their medications."[9] And that, "There is no threat to the public safety, and instead, the only conceivable harm is to Bayer's profits.

- In 2011 Dr. Eduardo Jose Guzman was accused of defrauding MediCal for inserting copper IUDs purchased from a Mexican supplier, rather than Teva. In his defense Guzman claimed that he did not understand the MediCal billing process, did not know that the FDA regulated IUDs, and that he purchased the IUDs from Mexico because they cost $150, as opposed to several hundred dollars for a ParaGard® IUD.[10] The court documents note that, "Until April 2006 MediCal paid $261.80 for each insertion of a ParaGard IUD. In April 2006 the payment increased to $374.16 per IUD. At the time of trial in August 2010, a single ParaGard® IUD cost $392."[11] The case was dismissed due to a deadlocked jury.

• In 2012 Dr. Bayardo Cruz got his medical license revoked after inserting Mexican IUDs but receiving partial refunds for Paragard® from Medi-Cal.[12] Cruz reported that ParaGard® costs approximately $300-400 to purchase, but he was only reimbursed $250 per device. Similar to Cope and Guzman, his clinic lost money with every IUD insertion.

• In 2013 Dr. James Buck was sentenced to 1 year of probation and paid $18,000 in fines for purchasing unapproved "foreign" Mirena® IUDs through a Canadian online pharmacy and then distributing them to his American patients.[13]

• By far the harshest case was suffered by Dr. Canh Jeff Vo, also in Kentucky, who was charged with health care fraud, mail fraud, misbranding, and smuggling for purchasing IUDs from a non-US supplier. His patients were quoted as saying, "You don't know what kind of side effects or what it's going to cause, if it causes you to not be able to conceive later on in life."[14] And, "Where can I get mine removed? I don't want Vo touching me ever again. He put one in me and if I can't trust that it is what it's supposed to be. I can't trust him at all." It's unclear where his patients got the idea that a Canadian IUD put them at higher risk for sterility. Dr. Vo faced a maximum of 233 years in prison, a fine of $3,010,000, and up to 3 years of supervised release.[15] Ultimately Vo pled guilty to the felony charge and paid over $75,000 in fines, but luckily escaped prison time.[16]

The incidences of "black market" IUDs have been cast in the local media as shameful examples of deception and greed on the part of the doctors, but that is a highly superficial reading of the events. A closer study of the doctors' actions within a broader global context reveals that these same actions, if they had occurred in one among several other countries, would be not only be ethical but completely ordinary, and it is in fact the US-specific context within which they have operated that must be judged as uniquely unethical.

First, the purchase of Mirena® IUDs from Canada were not technically of the "black market," and can be more accurately de-scribed as the "gray market," or more specifically, "parallel imports." The "black market" describes items which are illegal to sell and possess, such as cocaine. The term "gray market" broadly describes trade in any item which is legal to possess, but was ob-tained in an illegal manner. The term "parallel imports" specifical-ly describes the importation of a non-counterfeit product from an alternative source. Far from considered a part of the illicit black or gray market, parallel imports, under certain circumstances, are not only permitted in most European Union and many Asian countries, but are in some cases a legal obligation. For example, in Denmark, Germany, and Sweden, pharmacists are legally required to notify patients when cheaper versions of a prescribed drugs are available for parallel importation.[17] Germany requires pharmacists to pro-vide patients with cheaper drugs, unless specifically prohibited by the prescribing doctor. The Netherlands, Norway, Sweden, and the United Kingdom all offer incentives to encourage pharmacists to engage in parallel imports. By contrast, for the same behavior, doctors who engage in parallel imports in the United States risk earning a prison sentence. That parallel importers face such unusually stiff penalties in the US compared to other countries reveals far more about the US regulatory framework than it does about the action or the importers themselves.

Moving past the subjectivity in interpretation of the relative merits or evils of parallel imports, the primary failing of the Greedy Doctor Hypothesis lies in the doctors' purchasing choices. The vast majority of them purchased Mirena® IUDs from Canada for approximately $200 apiece, while copper IUDs can be purchased from multiple non-US providers for between $1 and $20. After a few hundred insertions any hypothetical Greedy Doctor could have made hundreds of thousands of dollars in profit off of the copper IUD arbitrage alone. Yet the doctors ignored this opportunity for high profit potential and instead paid up to a hundred times more for a Canadian Mirena® IUD. This choice would seem to imply that Greedy Doctors may be good at medicine but are horrible at math. More likely, that they chose to import Canadian Mirena® IUDs because they felt that the national classification was bureaucratic, not pharmacological, and that purchasing a familiar product from a legitimate—albeit Canadian—distributor did not compromise their patients' health. For example, these IUDs differed slightly and superficially from those approved by the American FDA, with differing thread lengths and with use instructions in another language, but the pharmacological components were identical. It's possible that a copper IUD purchased outside of the FDA-approved supply chain would be identical to a ParaGard® TCu380A, but it could not be said with as much confidence as for products that were produced by the same manufacturer as an approved device; that could only be said with certainly of the Mirena® IUDs.

Next, the supposedly Greedy Doctors' actions were the exact opposite of what normally occurs in the pharmaceutical gray market within the United States. In 2012 the Committee on Oversight and Government Reform released a report entitled, *Shining Light on the "Gray Market": An examination of why hospitals are forced to pay exorbitant prices for prescription drugs facing critical shortage.* The report investigated shortages that occur when pharmacies illegally sell their inventory to intermediaries, and concluded that:

> "[G]ray market companies that operate outside of authorized distribution networks take advantage of drug shortage situations to charge exorbitant prices for drugs used to treat cancer and other life-threatening conditions. Gray market drugs ...are sold to end users at aggressively marked-up prices. The questionable business practices of the distributors and pharmacies engaged in gray market sales result in higher health care costs and potential risks to patients."[18]

In these gray market circumstances it's local distributors selling the pharmaceuticals at an aggressively marked up price, effectively acting as drug scalpers so they can sell drugs back to hospitals for huge profits. In this context, the Greedy Doctors acted quite unstrategically by putting themselves at great legal risk to import drugs from outside the US to increase availability of medications at prices decreased from those which could be obtained through legal channels. Frankly, rather than serving to help interpret events, the Greedy Doctor Hypothesis makes them appear increasingly nonsensical.

The only media account which did not adopt the Greedy Doctor Hypothesis instead contrasted the FDA response to Canadian IUDs with the lack of prosecution in a concurrent event: the lethal adulteration of the blood thinner heparin. In 2008 a bad batch of heparin was related to 574 adverse events and 68 deaths in a 3 month period. It was later discovered that the heparin had been adulterated with oversulfated chondroitin sulfate (OSCS), which is a synthetic material that mimics some of heparin's chemical properties, but costs nearly 100 times less to produce. The FDA later concluded that the adulteration was likely to be financially motivated, as heparin is made from the mucosal tissue of pigs, and the event occurred in the Chinese supply chain during a period in which the country experienced a pig shortage. It is estimated that the adulterating party could have generated from $1 to $3 million dollars in profit from the adulteration. The Health Care Renewal blog reports:

> "Despite the facts that clearly patients died from receiving this adulterated drug, no individual has yet suffered any negative consequence for what amounted to poisoning of patients with a brand-name but adulterated pharmaceutical product.
>
> Yet everyone from state health departments to the federal authorities have jumped into the case of the unapproved IUDs imported, but from Canada, and apparently identical to the IUDs sold in the US. There is, at least so far, no evidence that the IUDs were defective or dangerous, and no evidence they have harmed patients. One doctor has been prosecuted for violating the Food, Drug and Cosmetic Act, and for health care fraud and money-laundering. No one working for Baxter International (or for the identified organizations within its supply chain) has been prosecuted for anything."[19]

It may not be accurate to directly compare these two events as if someone at the FDA made a conscious decision to *either* pursue "black market" IUDs *or* heparin adulteration. The disparity in prosecution between the respective incidents could be related to the relative simplicity in investigating domestic doctors and parallel imports versus following the pharmaceutical supply chain from Baxter International all the way to the Chinese active pharmaceutical ingredient manufacturers and suppliers—many of whom are unregistered chemical plants or peasant farmers scattered throughout the Chinese countryside.[20] But, the fact of the matter is that had the perpetrators been caught in the heparin adulteration, they, like the parallel importing doctors, would have been charged with violation of the Food, Drug, and Cosmetic Act.[21] That the FDA does not currently distinguish between a doctor who purchases an identical product from the same multinational company across the American border from someone who lethally adulterates a drug for a profit should be a matter of grave concern, particularly for well-intentioned, budget-conscious American healthcare practitioners.

Far from isolated to these events, the parallel importation of gray market IUDs from Canada is part of a much more prevalent phenomenon. The American demand for Canadian drugs is so large that Americans comprised a full 8% of the total Canadian pharmaceutical market in 2004.[22] Individuals are rarely prosecuted for the offense because border officials are permitted to exercise "enforcement discretion" for pharmaceuticals crossing the border, provided that they are not narcotics or controlled substances. This means that agents will typically not confiscate a personal stock of 3 months' supply of drugs from people crossing a US border, but lax enforcement does not change the fact that for Americans to obtain their prescription drugs from Canada is in fact against federal law.[23]

The battle over the right of Americans to purchase cheaper drugs from abroad is nothing new and has more or less been going on since parallel imports were first prohibited in 1987. In 2000 Americans scored a legislative victory with the Medicine Equity and Drug Safety Act of 2000, which was passed to allow pharmacists and wholesalers to reimport drugs back to the United States if they were being sold for lower prices abroad, provided that they had been manufactured in the US and approved by the FDA. However, in order to become law the act required a signature and certification from the Secretary of the Department of Health and Human Services (HHS); an event which never transpired. The act subsequently died in December of 2000, but the desire Americans had for buying cheaper drugs from abroad did not. A few years later the Pharmaceutical Market Access Act of 2003 (H.R. 2427) was introduced, which had provisions to allow the importation of drugs from 25 countries, including Canada, Australia, Japan, South Africa, and the European Union. The act passed in the House, was passed to the Senate after being modified to only allow the reimportation of FDA-approved drugs from Canada, but once again died due to lack of signature from the Secretary of the Department of Health and Human Services.

Then again in 2009 the so-called Dorgan amendment was introduced to, and subsequently rejected by, the Senate. If passed, the Dorgan amendment would have allowed Americans to purchase drugs from abroad, and saved an estimated $100 billion in prescription drug costs.[24]

When asked why they had voted down such a clearly beneficial amendment, American senators remarked that it had been in exchange for a deal with the pharmaceutical lobby organization Pharmaceutical Research and Manufacturers of America (PhRMA), to close the so-called "doughnut hole" in Medicare Part D. The "doughnut hole" is a colloquial term to describe a period in which seniors customarily exit the initial coverage of prescription-drug plan, and are then financially responsible for a higher cost of prescription drugs until he or she reaches the catastrophic-coverage threshold.

However, on the subject of the apparent Dorgan-for-doughnut trade which the Senate made, Ken Johnson, senior vice president for the Pharmaceutical Research and Manufacturers of America (PhRMA), said:

> "We have had absolutely no discussions with anyone in the Senate or the White House about how they plan to pay for closing the doughnut hole. It's a laudable goal, but we are already committed to providing a huge amount of money to help seniors who hit the coverage gap, and no one has asked us to date to provide any additional funding."[25]

At the point of this writing, the doughnut hole is in the process of being phased out, but is not expected to be eradicated until 2020. This laudable—albeit incremental—progress comes directly from the ACA, which again, speaks both for the necessity for, and insufficiency of, the healthcare act. Compared to the status quo, the eradication of doughnut hole, even if it takes a decade, or progress. Compared to the $100 billion savings that the Dorgan amendment would have brought had it not been rejected to placate the pharmaceutical industry, the progress brought on by the ACA begins to appear quite miniscule.

To his credit, in 2007 then-senator Barack Obama voted for the

Dorgan amendment. Subsequently, as president, when asked about pricing discrimination among the United States, Canada, and Mexico, remarked that, "Canada and Mexico are bulk purchasers of those drugs, so they negotiate much cheaper drug prices with the drug companies. We still don't do that, and I actually think it's something we should do – it would save us money...It may be that importation is still something we should look at in terms of further lowering the price of drugs."[26]

Indeed, the initial Senate draft of the Affordable Care Act included a provision to allow Americans to import drugs from Canada, but that provision was eventually dropped during negotiations with the pharmaceutical lobby. Shortly after, in 2011, senator Olympia Snowe (R-Maine) introduced S. 319, the proposed Pharmaceutical Market Access and Drug Safety Act of 2011, which would have allowed parallel importation from designated countries and additionally increased FDA inspection of offshore pharmaceutical manufacturing. This attempt was also unsuccessful. Still unwilling to admit defeat, three congressmen recently introduced bill called the Personal Drug Importation Fairness Act of 2013. If passed, this bill would allow Americans to buy medicines from Australia, Canada, Israel, Japan, New Zealand, Switzerland, South Africa, and countries in the European Union, but at the point of this writing its future is undecided. Another battle is currently being fought in the Supreme Court of Maine, over the right for insurance companies to cover pharmaceuticals purchased from abroad. The pharmaceutical lobby group Pharmaceutical Research and Manufacturers of America (PhRMA) sued the state of Maine, claiming that the bill is an "attempt to circumvent federal law,"[27] with no apparent cognizance of having correctly identified the strategy without its root cause: Americans are indeed trying to circumvent the law, after repeated failure to change it. Americans are increasingly frustrated by being legally required to pay exorbitant prices for equivalent products, and, indeed, are now trying to circumvent the law that has captured them. The particular case was dismissed in May of 2014, temporarily granting consumers in Maine a circumstance not unlike marijuana consumers in Colorado, with purchases that were legal according to local law yet against federal law. This is a highly precarious situation in which the difference in status as a law-abiding citizen or federal criminal can be a matter of juridical capriciousness. As of early 2015 this legal ambiguity appears to have been resolved, as this law was in fact overturned, once again returning Americans to the predictable homeostasis of being required to pay exorbitant fees for identical pharmaceuticals.

That's not to say that the right to purchase drugs from Canada is a panacea to America's distinct pharmaceutical problem. For one thing, the idea of Americans purchasing cheaper Canadian drugs is far less popular among Canadians than it is among Americans, in part because it places Canadians at risk for drug shortages or punitive pharmaceutical embargoes. For example, in March of 2003 UK-based GlaxoSmithKline cut sales to Canadian pharmacies that had been shipping cheaper drugs to America. Shortly after, another pharma giant, AstraZeneca, quickly followed suit.
[28] It has also been noted that, on the other side of the border, Mexico may be suffering from America's inability to control drug prices. Drug prices in Mexico tend to be far higher than would be expected considering the low income and general low price for goods in Mexico. One proposed explanation for this phenomenon is that prices have been raised in Mexico to reduce the incidence of illegal parallel imports to the United States. An OECD health

system report indicates that: "Manufacturers would rather forego some retail sales they could have had in Mexico than risk increasing the volume of US cross-border trade with Mexico (or increase pressure to allow parallel imports)."[29] That is to say, the very companies trusted to develop healthcare advances would rather provide medicine to fewer people at a higher price than increase access to their product if increased access may involve lowering product prices. Many have noted that in theory, increasingly globalized commerce should result in price convergence in which pharmaceutical prices would no longer vary across borders. In practice, legal institutions enforcing trade restrictions on identical products have potentially contributed to the poorest households in Mexico spending 30% of their disposable income on health, half of which goes to pharmaceuticals.[30]

There is an additional level of inequity to the globalization of medicine: at the same time that Americans have been fighting for the right to legally purchase prescription drugs from abroad but denied the right on the basis of safety, the pharmaceutical industry has quietly, and legally, been doing exactly what they've been lobbying against. That is to say, in the same time period that Americans repeatedly fought for the right to import cheap drugs from abroad, pharmaceutical companies prevented parallel imports based on claims that foreign drugs are unsafe, while simultaneously increasingly outsourcing pharmaceutical manufacture to foreign sites, often to places with low technological capacity and scant oversight, thereby increasing the circumstances that could make them unsafe. 2005 marked the first year that there were more foreign pharmaceutical manufacture sites than American sites registered with the FDA, and with each year domestic manufacturing sites continue to decline. [31] By 2007, nearly 70% of the world's active-drug-ingredient manufacturing sites were located in India or China,[32] and an estimated 40% of drugs consumed in the United States are now made abroad, with an additional 80 percent of active ingredients and bulk chemicals in US-manufactured drugs imported from abroad. [33] AstraZaneca's CEO has revealed a plan to potentially outsource all active-ingredient manufacturing within a few years. "If we can buy it cheaper than we can make it, then of course that's what we're going to do,"[34] said the CEO of GlaxoSmithKline, with no apparent sense of hypocrisy.

It's important to note that while a significant amount of product recalls and questionable practices in recent years have been related to the Chinese supply chain, the fact that China now supplies approximately 20% of all imported pharmaceuticals consumed in the US[35] without incident reveals that the vast majority of foreign manufacture sites are safe. Overall, the outsourcing of drug manufacture is not in itself a cause for concern. That being said, pharmaceutical industry and the FDA have long cited safety concerns as reasons for fighting parallel imports from Canada, yet of all the recent threats to US drug safety from abroad, not a single one came from Canada and all of them came with an FDA stamp of approval. It would be very easy for the United States to allow parallel imports from designated countries that have the same high safety standards that Americans expect, but to date none of the attempts to begin this process have succeeded.

In fact, considering that the European Medicines Agency (EMA) conducts regular inspection of manufacture sites, whereas China does not perform its own safety inspections and instead puts the burden of inspection upon the receiving country—to the end that the FDA only inspected approximately 5% of Chinese manufacture sites in 2009[36] and there are currently thousands of foreign sites that manufacture drugs for export to the US and *have never been inspected*—any arguments based on drug safety should actually *favor* parallel imports from designated countries. For example, a Pew white paper analyzing the heparin incident noted that, "China is home to the highest number of sites subject to FDA inspection outside of the United States…but receives the lowest levels of oversight compared with other countries…The emphasis on European inspections is surprising considering that regulatory oversight and standards for EU manufacturers are generally on par with those in the United States,"[37] and that, "Europe's *more robust* test specifications for heparin may have helped limit distribution of the adulterated drug there"[38] (emphasis mine). Allowing parallel imports from countries with the same amount of oversight Americans expect (but apparently don't always receive) for their drug supply would allow safety inspectors to stop duplicating efforts and free up resources for inspecting the areas with a greater oversight gap and pose a greater safety risk.[39] Put bluntly: we should not be wasting limited resources inspecting European-made drugs that have already been inspected by the EU, or banning drugs from Canada—we should be looking more closely at the flood of un-inspected production facilities in China.

The prohibition on parallel imports in the United States does not benefit American citizens, and moreover, it forces institutions to act against Americans' best interests. In the current status quo, American citizens are placed in a circumstance in which they are required by law to pay more money for equivalent products to no added benefit, and possible increased risk. Americans have tried to change these circumstances, and have been repeatedly unsuccessful. Medical professionals who prioritize providing their patients with affordable care are prosecuted to the full extent of the law, while people who profit from lethally adulterating drugs go uninvestigated and unpunished. Even if one does not explicitly conclude that the FDA has fallen into a circumstance of regulatory capture, it's quite clear that the current institutional structure of the US pharmaceutical regulatory framework effectively does a good job of protecting profits and a poor job of protecting people, a circumstance which represents quite a divergence from its initial purpose of ensuring consumer safety. Why do Americans assume their quite peculiar circumstances are normal, or in any way acceptable?

# NOTES

[1]     Carey (2009) pg 36

[2]     Lowes, Robert. Physicians Risk Lawsuits, Prison for
        Using Unapproved IUDs. Medscape.com. Published
        July 29, 2010. Accessed Dec 11 2013 from: http://
        www.medscape.com/viewarticle/725988

[3]     Beldon (2012)

[4]     St. James, Janet. Grapevine doctor defends using bargain
        IUDs. WFAA. Published Oct 21, 2010. Accessed Dec
        11, 2013 from: http:// www.wfaa.com/ news/
        health/Grapevine-doctor-defends-using-bargain-
        IUDs-105496683.html

[5]     Texas v. Women's Integrated Healthcare P.A. et al. Web11
        Dec 2013 from: https://www.oag.state.tx.us/newspubs/
        releases/ 2010/102110womens_healthcare_pop.pdf

[6]     FDA Consumer Health Information. FDA Cautions
        Against Using Unapproved IUDs. May 22, 2008. Web ac-
        cessed Dec 11 2013 from: http://www.fda.gov/downloads/
        ForConsumers/ ConsumerUpdates/UCM220033.pdf

[7]     Lowes (2010)

[8]     US Department of Justice Press Release. September 30,
        2011: Pine Bluff Doctor Sentenced in Health Care Fraud and
        Misbranding Case. Web accessed Dec 11 2013 from:

http://www.fda.gov/ICECI/CriminalInvestigations/ucm274435.htm

[9]     Lowes (2010)

[10]    The People v. Eduardo Jose Guzman, Defendant and Appellant; 2d Crim. No. B232299.

[11]    The People v. Eduardo Jose Guzman, Defendant and Appellant; 2d Crim. No. B232299.

[12]    Noah (2012), Perkes (2011), and Cruz (2012)

[13]    Herald-Leader (2013) and Safemedicines (2013)

[14]    Dickerson (2013)

[15]     US Attorney's Office Western District of Kentucky. March 21 2013

[16]    US Attorney's Office Western District of Kentucky. December 13 2013 [17]

        Docteur (2008) pg 114

[18]    Rockerfeller, et al. (2012)

[19]    Original quote from the Health Care Renewal Blog:

        http://hcrenewal.blogspot.com/2010/07/prosecut

        ing-doctors-for-importing-iuds.html

[20]    Pew (2011) pg 17 [21]

        Pew (2011) pg 15 and 53 [22]

        Docteur (2008) pg 11 [23]

        See Bhosle (2007), PBS (2003) and PBS (2013) for dis cussion of the Canadian/American importation situation.

[24]    See Dayen (2009) *Dorgan Amendment Slashed After Last-Minute PhRMa Deal PhRMa Hasn't Agreed To.*

[25]     See Grim (2010) Doughnuts For Dorgan: Drug Reim-
         portation Killed In Deal That Might Get Cheaper
         Drugs For Seniors.

[26]     See Rode (2011) Obama Interview Shows Americans
         Highly Concerned About Drug Prices; Drug Importa-
         tion Mentioned as Potential Solution.

[27]     See Charles Oullette et al. v. Janet Miller et al., Civil
         No. 1:13-CV-00347-NT

[28]     PBS (2003)

[29]     Docteur (2008) pg 173. The paper references Moïse
         and Docteur (2007), but others have hypothesized
         that proximity to the US has caused increased
         pharmaceutical prices for both Canada and Mexico,
         in an attempt to reduce the financial incentive for il-
         legal cross-border trade.

[30]     Docteur (2008) pg 138

[31]     Pew (2011) pg 21

[32]     Pew (2011) pg 22

[33]     Pew (2011) pg 7

[34]     Pew (2011) pg 22

[35]     Pew (2011) pg 23

[36]     Pew (2011) pg 46-48

[37]     Pew (2011) pg 47-48

[38]     Pew (2011) pg 39

[39]     In addition to the thousands of sites that have never

been inspected, Pew (2011) reports that foreign drug manufacture sites are currently only inspected once every 9 years on average, in contrast with domestic sites which are inspected once every 2-3 years (pg 8). Additionally, foreign inspections are generally much more lax, and surprise visits are rarely if ever done. Usually foreign sites are given up to a year's advance notice. If a foreign site fails an inspection, "resource constraints may mean the agency does not return for more than two years, if at all." The Government Accountability Office found that only 25% of noncompliant plants were reinspected, and 75% of those reinspected were found to have additional deficiencies (pg 47).

# CHAPTER 6
## THE CAMOUFLAGED ELEPHANT IN THE ROOM

" *[The healthcare bill is a] headlong rush into socialism.... we will not stand for the Obama-Pelosi-Reid hijacking of our freedom and democracy so they can impose their socialist 'utopia' of higher taxes, restricted access, inferior quality, and deadly inefficiency on the best health care system in the world.*"

> Michael Steele, Chairman of the Republican National Committee[1]

*"I really get annoyed every time I hear these talking heads talking about 'the government can't run anything'...Most veterans would give it a fairly good rating."*

> John Rowan, president of the Vietnam Veterans of America[2]

A t one point in time it was predicted that an increase in global trade would flatten the world, bringing about global convergence—a prediction that was only half-right. Products that are made and sold across the world are increasingly similar, but state enforcement of various pricing controls has helped ensure that they are not available for the same price; effectively resulting in a convergence of products with a divergence of prices. For example, the drugs that Americans illegally purchase from Canada are no different from the drugs they can legally purchase in the United States; frequently they're identical. The only difference between many Canadian drugs and American drugs are the prices, which are a product of the Canadian healthcare approach and public negotiation strategy. Because the only difference between these two products is the prices, it could be said that in fighting for the right to purchase identical drugs from Canada, Americans are, through their actions, implicitly revealing a preference for Canada's drug pricing controls and rejecting America's hands-off approach to pharmaceutical pricing.

What's the difference between policies in the United States and countries that achieve lower drug prices? It's the result of pricing systems employed by the governments, backed by the bargaining power of their respective public healthcare systems; one would not be as successful without the other. In essence, the pricing system is the brains and their market size is the brawn. The best example of this tag team might by the system of "reference pricing" designed by Germany in 1989, and now used by most EU countries as well as Australia, New Zealand, and Japan.[3] Reference pricing means that with each new drug approval a federal committee researches the drug and assigns it to a class of similar drugs. They then investigate how much other health systems pay for these drugs and adjust their own reimbursements accordingly. This does not constrain the price of the drug itself but rather how much the public insurer will pay for it, which affects its usage. For example, manufacturers can still price their products above the government-determined reference price, but if a consumer opts for a drug for which the manufacturer has set a price far above the reference price, the consumer is responsible for paying the difference between prices. In this way the public sector can manage costs incurred, and consumers can still exercise their preference for particular drugs, but only if they are willing to pay for the difference themselves.

Germany's pharmaceutical pricing system is fairly neutral in that assigns an average price among similar drugs, but does not comment on the quality of the drugs themselves, leaving that choice completely up to prescribers and consumers. By contrast, the UK's National Institute for Health and Care Excellence (NICE) employs what is called a "value-based" pricing system, in which the drug is evaluated on several factors such as cost-effectiveness and comparison to other available treatments, based on the criteria of Quality-Adjusted Life Years (QALY).[4] If a drug has the potential to considerably extend a patient's life, or improve the quality of life through a reduction in unpleasant side effects, it is said to bring an improvement of QALYs, and the manufacturer will be reimbursed more handsomely for it. If a drug is nearly identical to existing treatments, the manufacturer will not be highly reimbursed for it. In this way the United Kingdom has developed a multifaceted strategy to compensate manufacturers according to the added societal value of a medication above and beyond its market price, and additionally serves to reward medical innovation. Some American private insurers have recently begun to adopt their own system of value-based pricing, but for reasons that will be discussed shortly, despite some of them having a market share that exceeds the *entire population* of many of the EU nations that obtain lower pharmaceutical prices,[5] US private insurers are institutionally constrained from being able to match the low prices obtained in other countries.

Through strategies of cost-containment many countries have managed to provide a public system of universal healthcare to all citizens. The details of these strategies are very relevant in the context of the US battle for expanded medical coverage because any system that extends coverage to all citizens—or mandates that they purchase coverage—while failing to control prices dishonestly promises to attain the ideal of universal coverage while making no effective movement towards the mechanisms that actually make it possible.

There are many theories circulating to explain high US expenditures, which range from high usage,[6] to the commonsense explanation that spending is high because the prices are high.[7] I can't supply a complete answer to why American healthcare in general is so expensive, but I can explain some factors that certainly contribute to the problem in the case of pharmaceuticals.

First, it is indisputable that a major contributing factor to high drug prices in the US is that the Medicare is explicitly prohibited from negotiating lower prices. Shortly after President Bush signed The Medicare Prescription Drug, Improvement, and Modernization Act into law, economist Gerard Anderson was among the first to note that, "If the Medicare drug bill did not preclude Medicare from directly negotiating with drug companies, Medicare could probably obtain prices similar to those in other industrialized countries,"[8] and since then, many economists have come to agree. It's not clear *why* the federal government passed legislation specifically preventing itself from reducing its own Medicare expenditures, but it is clear that that move has contributed to higher pharmaceutical prices in the public sector, particularly to drugs that tend to be prescribed to senior citizens. For example, in order to test how the Medicare Part D expansion affected pharmaceutical pricing, two economists looked at drug prices just after the passage of the legislation, and compared the prices between drugs commonly used by Medicare users versus those not commonly prescribed to Medicare recipients. They found that in only three years, prices rose by 24.2% in drugs commonly used by the Medicare population, compared to a price rise of 18.8% in other drugs.[9] The Medicare Part D expansion in effect both gifted pharmaceutical companies with more customers,[10] and additionally allowed them to express their gratitude by disproportionately price-gauging them.

To be fair, Medicare only comprises one part of the US public health system, which together represents less than a quarter of the US population,[11] so it would not be fair to make generalizations which imply that Medicare-specific pricing mechanisms apply to the entire US pharmaceutical market. A quick explanation of similarities, differences, and sector intersections is in order.

The United States health system is divided into two sectors: the private and the public. The private sector is the system that is utilized by the vast majority of Americans, either through employment-based insurance or privately purchased plans. The American private sector employs a cost-control strategy infrequently seen in industrialized nations in that it doesn't employ one at all. Pharmaceutical companies in America are free to set prices at market entry at any price that they wish, and are free to raise prices as frequently as they like. Pharmaceutical prices in the American private sector are completely market-based and frequently monopoly-priced, in essence set at the maximum price the consumers and private insurance companies are willing to pay. Under normal circumstances market pricing eventually reaches a balance between suppliers trying to raise the price as high as possible and consumers seeking lowest possible prices through competition. However in the instance of American pharmaceuticals, suppliers are often given a monopoly on a product, and consumers and forbidden from purchasing from outside of the country, effectively inflating the prices considerably.

The only instances of pharmaceutical pricing regulation in America are in the form of mandatory discounts or rebates enforced by the public sector through the Medicare Part D program, the Medicaid Drug Rebate Program, or the Federal Supply Schedule (FSS). The FSS is a price set on behalf of federal entities such as the Veterans Administration or other eligible public health providers, and has two price levels: one that generally available to federal entities, as well as a lower Federal Ceiling Price (FCP), or "Big 4" price which is exclusively available to Department of Veterans Affairs, the Department of Defense, Public Health Service/Indian Health Service, and the Coast Guard. The pharmaceutical prices available to Medicare clients are required to be between 13% and 23% lower than the Average Manufacture Price (AMP) available in the private sector, and the FSS price is required to be at least 24% below the private sector AMP, and no higher than any "best price" offered to any other provider in the United States.[12]

Because the federal government mandates a pricing discount from pharmaceutical suppliers, some point to that as evidence that the United States has a system of pricing regulation which represents some degree of pricing control on the part of the American government. For example, a comparison of OECD pharmaceutical pricing policies noted that, "Although manufacturers in the United States can set list prices for new products freely at market entry, their freedom is checked, on the one hand, by de facto price regulation used in certain public programmes...and by competition among insurers in the private sector."[13]

This "de facto price regulation" has failed to control prices for two reasons: first, setting a public sector discount to constrain prices in a limitless private sector is about as effective as using a gondola to anchor a hot air balloon; certainly one is always below the other but the both rise together. Basing the public sector prices on an unregulated private sector has actually caused both prices to rise, rather than controlling the prices in either. This unintended consequence was acknowledged by the Congressional Budget Office to have been in effect as early as 1991,[14] but was nonetheless allowed to continue for nearly twenty years.

In 2010 the Affordable Care Act improved upon these circumstances, but only to a limited degree. At this point, if prices rise in the private sector faster than the rate of inflation, pharmaceutical companies are required to reimburse the federal government for the difference. This finally disincentivizes the practice of raising prices in the private sector for the specific purpose of legally raising prices to federal entities—such as when prices for drugs used most frequently by Medicare users rose faster than other drugs—but it does nothing to prevent prices being raised in the private sector overall. By contrast, Switzerland forces pharmaceutical companies to apply for permission before raising prices, and Canada limits pharmaceutical price increases to the rate of inflation. Now the US, like Canada, limits raising prices in the public sector to the level of inflation, but pharmaceutical companies can still raise prices in the private sector as much and as often as they wish. For this reason it is meaningless to say that there is a system of pricing control in the United States, because the system has utterly failed to control prices and has historically directly contributed to their upward flight.

Public and private sector pharmaceutical pricing is complex, but it can be made a little more accessible with concrete examples of prices, and in fact the FSS provides what is quite possibly the only publicly-accessible pharmaceutical pricing list in the United States.[15] Additionally the FSS provides a starting-point resource to observe the lowest prices available within the entirety of the United States. In other words, due to the complete lack of pricing transparency in US medical system, private citizens have no way of knowing how much *more* their private insurance company pays for certain pharmaceuticals than the FSS price, but it's impossible that the private company paid *less*. In this way the FSS can serve as an anchored reference point for the lowest possible price in American pharmaceuticals

The current FSS contract for ParaGard® was signed in 2008, with prices of $588.98 for general federal entities and, $352.42 for the Big 4. In 2007 Dr. James Trussell reported a private sector ParaGard® price of $494 which, if accurate, would either indicate that in practice, the Big 4 is the only federal entity that is offered any meaningful discount on the device, or that the price rose extremely rapidly between 2007 and 2008. Though incredible, the latter explanation is most likely accurate, as confirmed by a 2010 National Family Planning and Reproductive Health Association policy brief which reports that the federal 340B Drug Pricing Program experienced a price leap from $468 per unit to $703 per unit in a single month. The price reported in the National Family Planning and Reproductive Health Association brief refers to Mirena®, not ParaGard®, but is relevant to the context of both, as private sector prices for the ParaGard® tend to shadow those for Mirena® (recall the pricing graph in Chapter 4: In an IUDeal World). Additionally, as indicated in the Author's Note, when this book was initially written in 2014, the ParaGard® official website indicated that the price of a device was $754, but by January of 2015 the price had changed to $932, which represents a 30% price increase in one year. Unsurprisingly, the National Family Planning and Reproductive Health Association paper reported that federal Title X family planning grantees increased their spending on contraceptive supplies by an average of 26% in just three years.

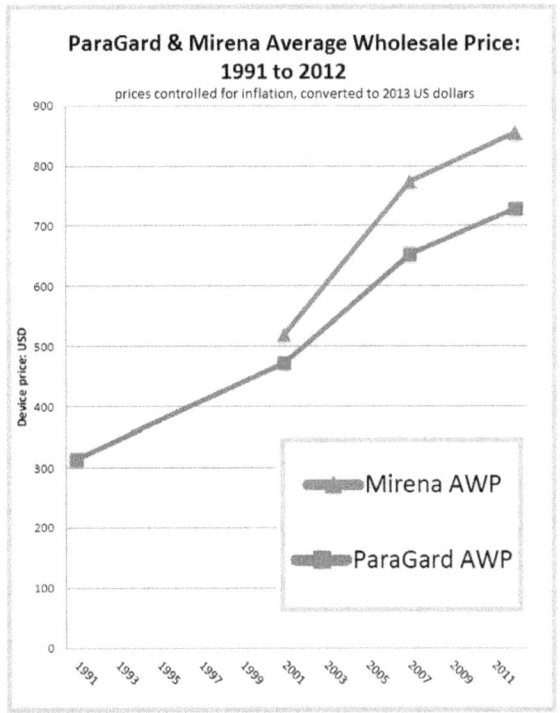

*Figure 8: See appendix C for data and sources.*

For Mirena®, the FSS contract was negotiated in 2012 and yielded prices of $637.87 and $502.05 for the general and Big 4 prices, respectively. By contrast to ParaGard®, The Mirena® Big 4 price of $502.05 represents a large 40% discount from Trussell's reported 2012 Average Wholesale Price of $844, providing an example in which the price to the private sector is *considerably higher* than the lowest possible federal government price. Knowing this, it's no wonder that physicians tried to order Mirena® IUDs from Canada when the FSS price available to most public clinics is $632.87, while the devices can be obtained for approximately $300 in Canada, or that the lowest price *in the entirety of the United States* for a copper IUD was $352.42—compared to approximately $50 in Canada, $20 in the UK, and a handful dollars elsewhere.

Because pharmaceutical prices are proprietary information not consistently accessible to the general public, it's difficult to construct a coherent map of the price change over time. The FSS provides current information but its applicability is severely limited, and research papers provide wider scope but in only sporadic increments. Nonetheless, mapping ParaGard® and Mirena® prices over time appear to suggest prevalence of the second unintended consequence acknowledged by the Congressional Budget Office: by requiring that the Big 4 be offered the "best price" among all favored suppliers, the private sector has responded by keeping prices high. Offering a low price to a private insurer would either have to result in a corresponding reduction in price to the Big 4, or be in violation of the Veterans Health Care Act of 1992. Put another way, the private insurance sector will never be able to beat American public sector prices, because to do so would be illegal. In this way, the claim that competition in the private sector results in a low prices is only true in a very limited capacity

If one were to judge the success or failure of American pricing policies based on results compared to the more rigidly controlled EU, it's quite easy to reach a verdict. In 2003 IMS Consulting compiled the prices of the top-100 reimbursed drugs in Switzerland and compared them with prices in other OECD countries. IMS found that prices in Switzerland were higher than all other European countries as well as Canada, but still lower than United

States FSS prices.[16] Put another way, the absolute *lowest* price that is legally obtainable to any entity within the United States—and unobtainable to most—is still *higher than the highest price* in Europe or Canada. It's additionally worthy of note that Switzerland, like the US, happens to be the only country in the EU that relies primarily on a private insurance sector rather than a public single-payer health system, and it also the EU country with the highest pharmaceutical prices.

Though the price difference between public and private sectors for an IUD in the US is higher than for most pharmaceuticals, it serves as an example—albeit an extreme one—of why millions of Americans may have given up on the public sector at home. Put bluntly: what's the point in fighting for a public plan if $588 for a sterilized piece of plastic and copper is the best it can do? The quiet but consistent illegal parallel importation of drugs from Canada or Mexico to the US indicates both that Americans are dissatisfied with the pricing system in their home country, but also that they are unwilling or unable to change it from within.

More broadly, the fact that the United States is the only OECD country besides Mexico and Turkey to not have achieved universal healthcare access by the 1990's[17] has led many people to believe that the US lacks support for the public integrated healthcare model—more commonly known as "single-payer" healthcare. This perception either ignores or is ignorant of the fact that the United States has had single-payer healthcare system in place since the 1930's, albeit one to which access is restricted to military personnel and eligible family members. The existence and mechanisms of the Department of Veterans Affairs (VA) and Veterans Health Administration (VHA) make it dishonest to simply claim that the US differs from most OECD countries in its lack of a single-payer public healthcare system. It is more accurate to say that the United States is bears the distinction of being the only OECD country to *have* a system of single-payer healthcare in place, and *still* neglect to provide universal healthcare coverage to all of its citizens

The purpose of discussing the VHA in the context of civilian lack of access to public health insurance isn't to imply that veteran benefits are undeserved or should be rescinded. Rather, it's to point out what could be described as a camouflaged elephant in the room: for nearly a hundred years demagogues and special interest groups have portrayed government assistance as "un-American," "socialist," or "Bolshevik,"[18] yet never do they address that the un-American socialist Bolshevik system is in essence the same to that which is extended to American soldiers; arguably the absolute last citizens that could credibly be described as "un-American." It begs the question of exactly what is so un-American about "socialized medicine," and upon which criteria—or which Americans—is the highly limited and subjective definition of what's "American" based?

The camouflaged elephant first entered the room in 1917, when government-commissioned articles denounced "German socialist insurance,"[19] in the same year that the War Risk law was amended to provide insurance against loss of life, personal injury, and government-subsidized life insurance for veterans.[20] This is the amendment which effectively set a course of action that resulted in the formal creation of the Veterans Administration which, by the 1990's, had become, "the single largest healthcare provider in the United States," handling 1.1 million hospital admissions per year and 24 million outpatient visits.[21] Nonetheless, the camouflaged elephant remains  to this day. For example, prior to the passing of the ACA several politicians lambasted it as "socialized medicine" and former vice presidential candidate Sarah Palin made the unsubstantiated claim that the healthcare bill included "death panels,"[22] apparently trying to conjure images of a healthcare system designed in a Soviet gulag.

The issues demagogues never specifically address are, if single-payer systems are inferior to private third payer, why do we offer an inferior system to our veterans? Or, conversely, if single-payer public healthcare is good enough for veterans, why isn't it good enough for civilians? The implicit answer is that there is absolutely nothing inferior or un-American about single-payer healthcare. In fact, in what has been called, "The greatest news story never told,"[23] the Veterans Health Administration consistently receives higher satisfaction ratings than the private health sector, among those who receive services. There is in fact little, if any, evidence to support claims that "socialized medicine" is inferior to privatized systems. The only thing that's un-American about other nations' single-payer universal healthcare is that they offer healthcare benefits to national citizens based on a belief that all people deserve healthcare, but by contrast Americans only qualify for single-payer healthcare if they are willing to risk their lives first. This is not to say that veterans should not receive some kind of additional compensation above and beyond what is available to civilians, but rather that Americans should question their system of veteran compensation in which, in exchange for risking their lives, veterans are offered the same basic benefits—such as healthcare and education—that are considered universal human rights in nations that are equally or even less wealthy than the US; and in order to make these rights appear as a benefit they are then rationed from the general American population.

Nonetheless, in its current incarnation it would be impossible to extend public healthcare to more American citizens. In a 2009 OECD working paper economists David Carey, Bradley Herring and Patrick Lenain pointed out that public sector health cashflows in the US are so uniquely high that for the same amount of total population per capita expenditure that the US spends to obtain health insurance for between 15-20% of its citizens, other OECD countries are able to offer universal insurance coverage to everyone.[24] In other words, one reason that the United States is unable to offer universal healthcare to all of its citizens is because US systems of public healthcare, such as Medicare, Medicaid, and the VA, are 5 times as expensive as other nations' public health systems.

There's absolutely no good reason for the United States to pay more for pharmaceuticals than any other industrialized nation. The United States has by far the highest population of any country in the OECD.[25] A monopsonistic (single-buyer) system would allow the United States to use its market power to obtain the lowest prices in the world, as opposed to the highest prices that it currently pays. But in order for that to work, the single-buyer would have to be empowered to flex its market muscle, not be constrained by inexplicable prohibitions against negotiation or meaningless pricing controls that both castrate the public sector and in fact cause prices in both sectors to rise uncontrollably.

Often in the United States market advocates will point to instances of government failure and use it as evidence that government intervention in general is to blame. This approach ignores that governments in just about every other developed nation besides the United States long ago succeeded in providing affordable healthcare to its citizens. A comparison of public health systems within and outside the United States indicates that government intervention is not an inherent source of failure; poorly implemented government intervention is. It's past time that we re-examined our entire paradigm.

# NOTES

[1]     Quote taken from Zimmerman (2010), initially from an email sent to supporters.

[2]     Quote taken from Jensen (2009)

[3]     For a detailed breakdown of German pharmaceutical policies, please see Paris (2008). For a general survey of OECD pharmaceutical pricing please see Docteur (2008).

[4]     An explanation of the QALY evaluation can be accessed from the NICE website here: http://www.nice.org.uk/newsroom/features/measuringeffectivenessandcosteffectivenesstheqaly.jsp

[5]     Docteur (2008) has noted that, "Several large publicly financed coverage schemes and private insurers in the United States have enrollments that exceed the populations of some OECD countries," (pg 15). Docteur additionally notes that The Veterans Health Administration has an enrollment of 7.9 million people, a number which exceeds the population of 1/3 of OECD countries (pg 87-88), though it only comprises of approximately 2% of the US population

[6]     Pharmaceutical usage is higher than average in the US, but not the highest. Docteur (2008) reports that France

and Spain are the OECD countries with the highest levels of per capita pharmaceutical consumption, followed by the US and Australia. The United States did spend the most money on pharmaceuticals, with a 2005 per capita expenditure of $792 USD PPP. This number is almost double the OECD average of $401 USD.

[7] Anderson (2003) has written that many popular and obscure economic hypotheses do not adequately explain uniquely high US healthcare expenditures, and has famously concluded that, "it's the prices, stupid."

[8] Anderson (2004)

[9] Frank and Newhouse (2008)

[10] Including pharmaceutical prescriptions in Medicare resulted in levels of drug utilization increasing between 11-70%, depending on the population (Berndt, 2010).

[11] DeNavas-Walt (2012) provides data (pg 75) indicating that only between 16.5 and 21.5% of the US population utilizes public health insurance. Docteur (2003) on pg 52 places the estimate closer to 25%

[12] Berndt (2010)

[13] Docteur (2008) pg 101

[14] The CBO report noted that, "Rather than continuing to give Medicaid access to the lowest prices available in 1991, manufacturers often chose to increase their best prices," and that, "During 1991, many of the FSS prices increased significantly, perhaps because of the best-price provision in the Medicaid rebate agreement."

[15]     Prices are publicly visible and can be searched here:
         http://www.va.gov/nac/index.cfm?template=Search_Pharmaceutical_Catalog

[16]     Docetur (2008)

[17]     Carey (2009) pg 21

[18]     Hoffman (2003)

[19]     Hoffman (2003)

[20]     The Depart of Veterans Affairs, VA History in Brief.

[21]     Daemrich (2011)

[22]     On August 7th, 2009 Sarah Palin posted from her
         Facebook page: "[G] overnment health care will not
         reduce the cost; it will simply refuse to pay the cost.
         And who will suffer the most when they ration care?
         The sick, the elderly, and the disabled, of course. The
         America I know and love is not one in which my
         parents or my baby with Down Syndrome will have
         to stand in front of Obama's 'death panel' so his bu-
         reaucrats can decide, based on a subjective judgment
         of their 'level of productivity in society,' whether they
         are worthy of health care. Such a system is downright
         evil." Palin is often credited with the words "death
         panels"—she never made it clear whom she was quot-
         ing in her update—but she did not invent the image of
         government-healthcare-as-executioner. On July 28th,
         2009 Representative Virginia Foxx said, "[The Repub-
         lican plan will] make sure we bring down the cost of
         health care for all Americans and that ensures afford-
         able access for all Americans and is pro-life because it
         will not put seniors in a position of being put to death

by their government." The perception that the ACA was "socialized medicine" and that it would cause the unnecessary death of Americans was well traveled in 2009, particularly in Republican circles, but has never been credibly explained or backed up by data.

[23]     Miles (2006)

[24]     Carey (2009) notes that, "Health expenditures per capita in the United States are by far the highest among OECD countries. The public share of health expenditure (46%) is much lower than in any other OECD country, except Mexico, but nevertheless public health expenditure per capita is higher than in most other OECD countries. For this amount of expenditure in the United States, government provides insurance coverage only for the elderly and disabled (through Medicare, which primarily insures persons aged 65 or over and individuals with disabilities and end-stage renal disease) and some of the poor (through Medicaid and the State Children's Health Insurance Program (SCHIP)), whereas in most other OECD countries this is enough for government to provide universal primary health insurance."

[25]     The United States has the highest population in the OECD, with approximately 313 million people in 2012. The next highest population is less than half that number, with the 127 million people that live in Japan. The collective European OECD population exceeds USA's just slightly, with a combined population of 332 million, but it takes 17 countries to comprise that total. Population statistics derived from: http://stats.oecd.org/

# CHAPTER 7
## THE DIAGNOSIS IS CLEAR; THE CURE IS UNCERTAIN

*"[W]e did not develop this product for the Indian market, let's be honest. We developed this product for Western patients who can afford this product, quite honestly."*

Marijn Dekkers, CEO of Bayer[1]

*"A framework that relies upon private marketing monopolies is morally repugnant, economically inefficient and corrupt. We can and should do better."*

Love, et al. Make drugs affordable: replace TRIPs by R&D-plus. 2004

At this point it's well established within the literature that tying pharmaceutical funding to market performance has perverted the incentives of the pharmaceutical industry, skewing their priorities towards sales over patient welfare. For example Dr. Ben Goldacre has written about the high incidence of pharmaceutical companies neglecting to publish unfavorable research, even for drugs that were known to increase suicidal behavior in pediatric patients. After GlaxoSmithKlein was investigated to ascertain the degree to which the company knew that their drug, Paxil, had a tendency to increase suicidal thoughts and actions in pediatric patients, an internal document was found that said, "It would be *commercially unacceptable* to include a statement that efficacy [in children] had not been demonstrated, as this would undermine the profile of paroxetine."[2] (emphasis mine) That is to say, company executives were fully aware that the drug was not effective and potentially dangerous to children, but made a conscious decision that it would be better to put children at risk, instead of their profits.

In *Sex, Lies, and Pharmaceuticals: How Drug Companies Plan to Profit from Female Sexual Dysfunction*, Ray Moynihan and Barbara Mintzes have additionally written about unethical "disease mongering", which is a term commonly used to describe the post hoc invention of a disease or diagnosis to suit an existing treatment, rather than the more desirable process of finding cures to known and problematic diseases. In their book, Moynihan and Mintzes traced the invention of "Female Sexual Dysfunction", through which several pharmaceutical companies applied millions of dollars to solving the particular medical problem of how to convince women to buy treatments for erectile dysfunction.

More generally, two separate former editors of academic medical journals have publicly spoken out against the consequences of pharmaceutical profit-seeking behavior, one claiming that medical journals have become, "an extension of the marketing arm of pharmaceutical companies."[3] Additionally, Economists Boldrin and Levin have written that the profits related to market exclusivity encourage secrecy and discourage collaboration among researchers, to the detriment of innovative medical discoveries. [4] And the tendency for pharmaceutical companies to ignore diseases that mostly affect the poor is so well-known that it has a name: the, "90/10 gap"—so named because 90% of research funding goes to research diseases that affect 10% of the global population. Taken collectively, the big picture indicates that the pharmaceutical industry is currently suffering from a strong case of perverse incentives. This is not a new revelation, nor is it credibly in dispute; what remains to be seen is what—if anything—will be done to cure it.

The IUD provides evidence of an additional manifestation of perverse incentives in the market-based pharmaceutical industry: a bias against durable, economical solutions. As mentioned in Chapter 2, The IUD goes MIA, the United States lost IUD access in the 1980's due to reduced consumer demand and liability concerns. At one point it appeared that Europe might also suffer an IUD shortage, but for a very different reason than in the United States. In 2000, Ortho Pharmaceuticals had announced that they would stop production of the Gyne T 380 slimline—a variation of the TCu380A available in Canada and Europe. Dismayed doctors were prompted to write a letter to the The Lancet, a prominent medical journal, decrying the "tragic paradox" that "the world's most effective copper IUD" and the "method that nearly achieved" the worldwide goals of, "safe, cheap, long acting, and effective contraceptive" would no longer be available.[5] The doctors' concerns turned out to be unfounded, as the TCu380A remained on the European and Canadian market through other distributors. But they had raised a good question: "Should profitability determine the availability of effective contraception?"

Ortho Pharmaceuticals did not have a Dalkonesque disaster on their hands, nor were they in the same litigious environment as the United States. Reliable contraception was then, and will always be, highly in demand due to the fact that nearly all women use it at some point in time, and that the average woman devotes approximately thirty years of her life to avoiding pregnancy. Moreover, Canadian and European women have historically used IUDs at much higher rates than American women. Frankly, the potential market demand for this item is any profiteer's dream. How could one of the world's best contraceptive methods not be profitable?

Ironically, the profit potential for the TCu380A product is undercut by the robustness of the product. The average American woman wants approximately two children[6] and the TCu380A can function for over 10 years—possibly up to 20.[7] Even if a woman used IUDs exclusively as the only method of contraception ever used in her entire life, she would only ever need a total of approximately three devices; to a collective product manufacture price that does not exceed $1. This product—regardless of demand—has an inbuilt low potential for repeat customers or profit. The only way to extract maximum profits from this device is to raise the price as high as possible, even at the expense of drastically reduced consumption—which is exactly what Bayer and Teva have done in the United States. As we've seen, there are not enough reproductively-aged women in all of the United States to compensate for lost profits if the devices were marginally priced. It appears that when monopolistic suppliers are permitted to price goods at will, the more effective a medical device is, the more expensive—and scarcer—it will be.

To be clear, there is absolutely nothing inherently wrong with high profits in an industry as socially important as medicine. However, at this point in time there is a distinct lack of evidence to support a direct connection between the amount of money a pharmaceutical companies earns and the quality of output it produces in return. In fact, in 2006 The Congressional Budget Office observed that, "Continued growth in R&D spending has appeared to have little effect on the pace at which new drugs are developed," and that, "Measured by the number of drugs approved per dollar of R&D, the innovative performance of the drug industry appears to have declined."[8] Others have criticized the industry more directly, nothing that over the past few decades pharmaceutical income andpurported R&D spending has increased considerably, but pharmaceutical innovation has continued at a constantrate.[9]

In addition to perversely incentivizing unethical or un-productive behavior, a major problem with the state of so-called Big Pharma's handling of finances as it currently stands is that it's massively inefficient. The average pharmaceutical company allocates approximately 5% of its expenditures on medicine pro-duction, 15% on R&D[10] and an additional 30% on marketing. In particular, an industry report released in 2011 indicated that Bayer and Teva spent 8% and 5% of their 2008 revenues on R&D, respectively.[11] That pharmaceutical companies spend at least twice as much on marketing as they do on R&D indicates that if they did not need depend on market sales for funding, they could potentially triple the amount of money spent on R&D without rais-ing the prices of drugs. Further, it means that when people ratio-nalize that high drug prices are justified by higher R&D funding, they also need to factor in that for every one of their dollars they provide for R&D, they're also providing approximately twice as much to the marketing budget, which more often than not goes towards paying drug representatives to mislead doctors.[12]

In any discussion of the role of marketing in the pharmaceu-tical industry it's important to note that the majority of marketing expenses do not go towards direct-to-consumer advertising, but rather towards the "sales force"—more commonly called "drug reps." Drug Representatives' professional responsibility is to develop relationships with doctors in hopes of influencing their prescribing decisions. As much as 75% of a pharmaceutical company's marketing budget can be directed towards drug reps, to the point that there is now 1 drug rep for every 4-7 doctors, with doctors being visited by as many as 29 drug reps per week.[13] That doctors are receiving this many visits from drug reps is especially alarming because in 1995 researchers observed that 11% of the information that drug representatives provided to doctors was false, all of it flattering their sponsoring drug, and alarmingly, physicians failed to notice the inaccuracies.[14] A meta-analysis of 255 journal articles found that most physicians believe that they are not affected by drug reps, but evidence indicates that drugs reps have a heavy influence on prescriptions, and hospital formularies, including inappropriate and unnecessarily expensive drug prescriptions.[15] Other studies have found that the more gifts a physician receives from drug reps, the more likely the physician is to believe he or she is not affected by them, even though evidence clearly indicates that it does.[16] Because there is no evidence to support that information from the drug reps is helpful, and ample evidence to suggest it is harmful, the meta-analysis urged physicians to, "follow the precautionary principle and thus avoid exposure to information from pharmaceutical companies unless evidence of net benefit emerges."[17] However, there is currently little reason to believe that this advise has been sufficiently well-heeded.

Past the fact that pharmaceutical companies devote more money to drug reps than they do to R&D, it's increasingly clear that the amount of money that goes towards productive R&D is even lower than 15% of  expenditures. For example, it's a well-established medical fact that the vast majority of industry-funded research flatters the sponsoring drug.[18] In order to believe that these results—which nearly infallibly demonstrate the superiority of the product that is paying for the trials—present an accurate and unbiased description of medicine, one would have to believe that the pharmaceutical industry is so good at creating perfect drugs that they hardly need to conduct research at all. That is of course absolutely incredible and can easily be dispelled by the multiple findings that a significant amount of research never gets published. Goldacre has the following to say on the subject:

> "If we were talking about one single study, from one single group of researchers, who decided to delete half their results because they didn't give the overall picture they wanted, then we would quite correctly call that act 'research misconduct.' Yet somehow when exactly the same phenomenon occurs, but with whole studies going missing, by the hands of hundreds and thousands of individuals, spread around the world, in both the public and private sector, we accept it as a normal part of life."[19]

Issues of ethics and misconduct issues aside, it's clear that it's simply not true to assume that all research and development expenditures are used constructively to design new treatments. It appears that a significant amount of R&D is essentially more marketing in disguise—researching the right question to ask and developing new market strategies. Researcher Donald Light has estimated that pharmaceutical companies realistically only devote about 1% of their expenditures to original, basic medical research. [20] If accurate, that would indicate that pharmaceutical companies are no more efficient than the federal government—which devotes approximately 1% of the budget to funding National

Institute of Health research.[21] But presumably no one has ever argued against lowering taxes based on the supposition that it would result in decreased medical research, as some do when the subject of purchasing cheaper pharmaceuticals from abroad comes up.

There have been some innovative attempts rectify the power markets have to pervert incentives in the pharmaceutical industry and allocate funding more appropriately, such as the so-called "prize" system. This system is designed to realign incentives, as well as break up the increasingly vertical monopolies in the pharmaceutical industry—monolithic companies that research, test, manufacture, and market pharmaceuticals at their own discretion. Under a prize system patents would either be eliminated or auctioned off, and financial rewards would be paid directly to the research entities responsible for medical innovation, essentially genericizing all pharmaceutical manufacture. This would lower costs by eliminating the, "shadow tax of the patent system—monopolistic price minus marginal cost."[22] At this point the potential reach of the "shadow tax" should be very obvious to readers of this book: approximately $932 less 25 cents, in the case of copper IUDs. Additionally prizes reward innovators at the time of, and to levels proportionate to, the innovation, rather than allowing a circumstance in which monopolistic suppliers are able to wring maximum profits from a hundred thousand percent markup of a medical device which has not been innovated in 40 years—to use the example of IUDs.

Another point worth mentioning is that savings through generic medicines is one arena in which the American faith in the market system is justified. As mentioned in the previous chapter, America tends to have the highest pharmaceutical prices in the world—

diseases that is, for drugs that are still on patent, which allows manufacturers to set prices at will with no fear of competition. However, for off-patent generic medicines America has some of the lowest prices.[23] In this way the price trajectories of patented medicines versus generic medicines serves as a microcosm of elementary economic theory: monopolies cause prices to be very, very high, and competition causes prices to be very, very low— but only if the playing field is level and filled with lots of competitors.

An additional benefit of the prize system is that it confronts global inequality in a realistic way. It's well-known that the vast majority of R&D funding comes from the richest countries, and for that reason some people believe that by offering pharmaceuticals for a cheaper price, poor nations are unfairly being subsidized by rich countries.[24] This approach is absolutely nonsensical. According to the Credit Suisse Global Wealth Report, 90% of the world's population has wealth that is under $100,000 USD.[25] That means that 90% of the world will never be able to afford— to use a recent headline as an example—to pay between $60,000 to $96,000 for a year's supply of Nexavar, Bayer's newest cancer treatment.[26] They will either buy it for $176 a month from Natco, an Indian generic manufacturer, or they will go without it. In 2012 Bayer filed an appeal with Indian Patent Office to prevent Natco from supplying the drug in India, but Bayer recently lost the appeal. Bayer has released a statement indicating that India's decision, "weakens the international patent system and endangers pharmaceutical research."[27]

In order for India's decision to weaken research, there would have to be reason to believe that Natco is attracting customers that would have otherwise bought drugs from Bayer. According to Credit Suisse, 94.4% of India's population has a net worth of under $10,000 USD and an additional 5.2% have wealth between $10,000 and $100,000.[28] With 99.6% of India's population unable to afford Bayer's Nexavar prices, it's unclear how they expected to get money that doesn't exist from the Indian market. Preventing Natco from distributing the product does not direct sales away from Natco and towards Bayer, it simply prevents people from accessing the drug at all. The prize system is superior to the patent system in that it acknowledges global income inequality in a realistic way in that it allows richer countries to subsidize medical research—which they are already doing and will continue to do until global economies converge—without encouraging pharmaceutical companies to engage in the decidedly un-Hippocratic behavior of fighting to withhold treatment from the sick.

The only way pharmaceutical companies could potentially be losing sales to developing nations is if relatively wealthier people find themselves in a position where their insurance does not cover an expensive treatment, and subsequently decide to travel to a country where it is done well and cheaply—so-called "medical tourism." As opposed to the utter fantasy that Natco might be siphoning developing-nation clients that would have otherwise paid for Bayer's treatment, losing patients to medial tourism is a realistic concern. In 2007 there were very few books on the subject; how-to guides designed to advise American medical consumers on the costs, benefits, and risks of obtaining medical treatment outside of the United States. By the end of 2013 Amazon.com had nearly 50 titles listed—a twenty-fold explosion in just over 5 years. The market has grown rapidly in size, scope, as well as complexity. The earlier titles are simple guides for individuals, crude in comparison to later developments. 2010 marked the emergence of how-to guides designed for institutional stakeholders, such as insurers, and facilitators—a new breed of medical travel agents. Most recently, the field has changed with American politics, with two early-2014 titles designed to assist employers in offering international insurance packages to their employees;[29] a direct response to changes brought about by the Affordable Care Act. Medical tourism is the inevitable consequence of the extreme price discrimination in healthcare between the United States and other countries and, short of forbidding sick people from leaving the country, there's absolutely no way to prevent it. However, allowing medicinal prices to converge by removing patents and genericizing the pharmaceutical industry would remove the incentive to do so.

The prize system has been intellectually debated since the nineteenth century, but recently been attracting so much intellectually serious support that it has earned, "thousands of pages in law reviews and economics journals" not to mention the attention of, "Nobel laureates, newspaper editorialists, and presidential candidates."[30] Within the US political sphere, Congress has seen a bill proposed by Senator Bernie Sanders which would determine the prize fund by a set percentage of GDP. The Medical Innovation Prize Fund Act was presented to Congress in 2011, but was not enacted.

Critics of the prize idea point towards the complexity of implementation. For example, the granting committee will be charged with making decisions regarding which innovations are more valuable than others. Marilyn Wei has asked: "Is a drug that decreases the likelihood of anxiety in someone with social anxiety disorder more or less socially valuable than a drug that incrementally improves the eyesight of the minority of elderly patients? ...

How does one compare the health impact of drugs that saves patients in the Japanese population, who have a higher average lifespan, compared to saving African patients, who may then later die from other diseases?"[31] While valid, arguments against the prize system on the basis of inherent imperfection to the system ignore that these decisions are already being made involuntarily. The current reward system effectively determines that drugs which cater to the richest people in the world are more valuable than those that would confront the issues—even those that concern life or death—that primarily affect the billions who live in developing nations. A market-based reward system inherently results in a pharmaceutical industry that is decidedly unjust, not to mention undemocratic and in essence a de facto pharmaceutical plutocracy.

Other critics have noted that the prize system has yet to be proven more effective than the patent system.[32] This criticism has embedded within its logical structure a fairly absurd tautology. In order to provide a stronger incentive than drug patents, the prize system would have to be offer at least equivalent, if not increased, financial rewards. A well-implemented prize system could continue to provide pharmaceutical research firms with hefty profits, but it would have the benefit of requiring them to actually produce something socially valuable to earn it—something that is not a requisite in the current patent and market system. As of yet prizes are rare and in minuscule amounts compared to earnings of billion dollar blockbuster drugs on the American market. To discredit an idea that has neither been tried nor tested on the basis that it has not yet proven itself misrepresents the very purpose of research and experimentation itself.

Further, the patent system has reigned primarily due to a long history that extends to the feudal system—but historical precedent doesn't equate superiority. In fact, in the field of advanced medical discoveries, it's usually antithetical. Economist Dean Baker has noted that, "It is widely recognized that, left to itself, the market will not support an adequate amount of bio-medical research—companies that pay for research will not be able to recoup their research expenses if they sell their products in a competitive market".[33] Donald Light has extended Baker's argument to observe that, "The global press network never tells audiences about the detailed reconstruction of R&D costs for RotaTeq and Rotarix that found costs and risks were remarkably low up to the large final trials, and that concluded the companies **recovered their investments within the first 18 months**"[34] (emphasis mine). Slowly, the economic consensus appears to be that some sort of government intervention is necessary in order to ensure that pharmaceutical companies recoup their R&D investment, but the patent system is increasingly appearing inappropriate.

Some of the harshest criticism of the prize idea comes from the very person who sponsored The Medical Innovation Prize Fund Act. "This is a very radical idea and one that will most certainly not be passed in the short term." Senator Sanders has said. Yet he also concluded, "However, it is a concept that is absolutely right, that must be passed, and will be passed when the American people demand it."[35]

Indeed there is an additional reason why the American people should demand a reform to the pharmaceutical market as it currently stands. High amounts of consumption compounded with record high prices have contributed to the United States representing the largest pharmaceutical market in the world. Estimates vary by researcher and year, [36] but in general the

United States market constitutes between one third and half the entire global pharmaceutical market. For example, in 2008 an OECD report estimated that 80% of the value of global drug sales comes from only 9 countries, with the US representing 45% of the global share.[37] The next largest market was Japan at a mere 9%, followed by France (6%), Germany (5%), and the UK (4%). With an economic significance ten times larger than any other country, the single largest source of pharmaceutical profits, and the only significant market-based system in the world, if the priorities of the pharmaceutical industry can be said to have been perversely incentivized, America is clearly the source of the perversion. Consequently, America is the only country that can remedy it.

# NOTES

[1]     This quote is well-traveled. One of many places in which it can be found is Gokhale (2014)

[2]     Perverse incentives and unethical behavior was a major topic in Ben Goldacre's book, Bad Pharma: how drug companies mislead doctors and harm patients. Quote taken from Chapter 1.

[3]     Smith (2005). Additionally, Marcia Angell is a former editor of the New England Journal of Medicine, and has made similar accusations.

[4]     Boldrin et al. (2008), Chapter 9

[5]     Milsom et al. (2000)

[6]     Gold (1998), Guttemacher (2013b)

[7]     Sivin (2007)

[8]     The Congressional Budget Office (2006)

[9]     Boldrin (2008), Light (2012)

[10]    Chandrasekaran (2003) reports the following pharmaceutical value chain cost distribution: R&D, 15%; Primary manufacturing cost, 5-10%; secondary manufacturing/packaging, 15-20%; marketing/distribution, 30-35%, general administration, 5%. Cited in Kumar (2006). Elsewhere in the report Kumar reports that the

average pharmaceutical company spends approximately 2.5 times more on marketing than they do on R&D. An industry report prepared by IMAP (2011) did not comment on marketing expenses but indicated that, "Manufacturing costs for proprietary drugs are negligible — at 3 percent to 5 percent of the ex-factory price for chemical drugs, and typically below 20 percent for biotech drugs," and listed several pharmaceutical companies that spent less than 10% of their sales revenue on R&D, though most spent between 13%-20%. Similarly, Creese (2004) pg 17 indicates that Merck only spent 5% of their sales revenue on R&D, but an industry paper (IMAP 2011) reports that in 2009 Merck spent 20% of revenues on R&D.

[11]    IMAP (2011)

[12]    Kumar (2011)

[13]    Pew Prescription Project (2009)

[14]    Zieglar et al. (1995)

[15]    Spurling (2010)

[16]    Hodges (1995), Katz (2003)

[17]    Spurling (2010)

[18]    Goldacre (2013) devoted an entire chapter to justifying this statement and provided multiple resources. Rather than reproduce his entire volume I refer skeptics to his work.

[19]    Goldacre (2013)

[20]    Light et al. (2012)

[21]     The United States spends approximately 1% of the federal budget on National Institute of Health research. US Senate, Joint Economic Committee (2000).

[22]     Hemel et al. (2013)

[23]     Docteur (2008) pg 78 discusses several studies on comparative drug prices. Results vary depending on the drugs studied, but most find that the US has the highest prices in the world on name brand, innovator drugs —though one has placed the US second to Japan, and another placed the US in third compared to Japan and Mexico. By contrast, many studies have also found that the US has among the lowest prices for generic drugs, but also that the price of generic drugs does not lower the price of innovator drugs. Because the US is a country of extreme price outliers, any study which compares drug prices must be analyzed carefully to see which data is included.

[24]     Mark McClellan, one-time FDA commissioner has frequently commented that other nations unfairly use market power to lower the prices of drugs, causing America to subsidize R&D disproportionately. Similarly, a US Department of Commerce report (US DoC, 2005) claimed that US citizens would benefit in the long term if other countries were to deregulate prices and allow the free market to operate. A pertinent absence in the DoC report is that it rightly observed that high cash flows lead to higher R&D spending, but it made no comment on the reduced amount of pharmaceutical output in the face of increased spending in the past

decade, nor on the inefficiency of receiving only approx-imately a 15% R&D return. Light (2005) has traced the origins of the "free rider myth" to the late 1990's, "as a response to a grass roots movement started by senior citizens against the high prices of essential prescription drugs."

[25]    Suisse (2013) pg 22

[26]    See Gokhale (2014), Herper (2012), and Rumman (2013) for news articles pertaining to the Bayer/Natco case. Ahmed (2013) reported that Nexavar cost $5,181 a month in India, which would be a total of $62,172 a year. Herper (2012) listed an American annual price of $96,000.

[27]    Rumman (2013)

[28]    Suisse (2013) pg 49

[29]    Okoye (2014), Todd (2014)

[30]    Hemel et al. (2013)

[31]    Wei (2007)

[32]    McArdle (2013)

[33]    Baker (2008)

[34]    Light et al. (2011)

[35]    Gaffney (2012)

[36]    Boldrin (2008) claims that drug sales in the US account for about 48% of the total, followed by Europe's 29% and Japan's 11%. A report by the World Health Or-ganization (Creese, 2004) reports that in 1976 the USA comprised of 18.4% of world drug sales, 28.1% in 1985,

and 52.9% in 2000; in every year listed the US was the top consumer. IMS data indicates that in 2009 the US comprised of 35.9% of the world market, followed next by the entire European continent (31.5%), then the combined areas of Asia (excluding Japan), Africa, and Australia (12.7%), next Japan (11.3%), Latin America (5.7%), and lastly, Canada with a at 2.8% share. In 2011 an industry report (IMAP, 2011) indicated that the US comprised of 28% of global pharmaceutical sales in 2009, with Europe at only half that, with a 15% market share, followed by Japan's 12% share. In short, exact proportions vary but the US is always shown to be the indisputable pharmaceutical industry honey pot.

[37]     Docteur (2008) pg 11

# CONCLUSION
## ASK YOUR OWN STUPID QUESTIONS

*"[O]ne should look for power not in controversy but in silence...controversy reveals fissures in power, and signifies a topic beyond the real concern of power, an erosion of power, or conflicting powers in which neither party is able to subjugate the other. In issues around which there is overwhelming power, there is no legitimate controversy, only silence, because discourse beyond the specified boundaries is not 'controversy' but 'craziness.'"*

Lant Pritchett. The Cliff at the Border. 2006[1]

*"We have a health-care system that reflects our national values. It's highly individualistic, entrepreneurial, and suspicious of centralized supervision. In practice, Medicare and private insurers impose few effective controls on doctors' and patients' choices. That's the way most Americans want it."*

Robert Samuelson. Obama's Healthcare Headache.[2]

M odern democracies are structured around the notion that the kinds of people who are attracted to positions of power are exactly the people who require supervision upon obtaining it.[3] A properly-functioning system of checks and balances ensures that, in their brief tenures in power, many politicians manage to avoid completely destroying the country—

in fact, sometimes they manage to leave it in better condition than it was in when they found it. Democracy is, in the famous words of Winston Churchill, "the worst form of government—except for all those other forms that have been tried from time to time." Capitalism is exactly the same. There's nothing wrong with harnessing people's natural tendencies towards self-interest in order to obtain a wide range of pro-social outcomes, including the field of medicine. However, business interests, like ambitious politicians, should always be closely supervised, and should never be unquestioningly given too much latitude to control a nation's infrastructure.

When I first started this project, I only wanted to know what it was that I didn't understand about plastic and copper that justified the nearly thousand dollar price tag of a copper intrauterine device. Was it a certain type of plastic, or copper that had to undergo a special process? Yes. The copper IUD is made of low density polyethylene with barium sulfate mixed in so that it can be seen through an X-ray, then oxygen-free electronic (OFE) 99.99% pure copper is added to the stem and arms, and the unit if gamma-ray sterilized. The copper IUD is indeed constructed under very precise specifications, but it is nonetheless constructed for approximately twenty cents. In other words, Dr. Espey did exaggerate somewhat when she quipped that the copper IUD could be made from materials at Home Depot for less than 5 cents, but she was not terribly far off.

If the materials of the IUD do not justify its expense, something about its context must. In order to get a proper understanding of the IUD's current place in America, I needed to understand its place in the rest of the world. That led me to see that the copper IUD does not need to cost a thousand dollars, and in fact has a price that is quite variable. It can cost anywhere from $0.31, to $2, all the way up to several hundred dollars. The IUD's history in America was illuminating. For example, it indicated that a medical device's price can multiply several times over without experiencing a drop in consumer demand—something referred to as "price elasticity". That the price of the IUD can triple while simultaneously experiencing a tenfold increase in use indicates that women's demand for reliable and durable contraception is highly inelastic—not to mention financially exploitable, in the absence of protection from said exploitation.

At this point it became very important to note which questions were being asked, and which weren't. Are IUDs among the most reliable forms of contraception? Yes. Are IUDs, if used for several years, more economical than most competing forms of birth control? Yes. Are IUDs a more economical expenditure in public funds than a Medicaid-birth? Of course. It is quite easy to find research credibly justifying these answers to these questions. Absent from the literature is: How much money have private citizens, not to mention federal and state governments, spent on a device that costs exponentially more in the US than it does in other parts of the world? How much public waste and social harm has been caused by a simple contraceptive being prohibitively expensive to the people that need it? At what point does profit-maximization in medicine cost more than it provides? At what level must excess reach before inefficiency in the private sector and deficits in upholding monopolies for medicine are readily acknowledged in the national discussion?

Although not in reference to contraceptives and the IUD, the last question is one that has been asked by many Americans in recent years, with increasing frequency. Americans were promised that the American way of capitalistic competition in the private sector would lead to lower prices and more efficiency. They were not told that several factors unique to the medical industry make fair competition, and thereby lowered prices, impossible.

Foremost, there's the issue of safety. Truly fair competition would require many players, which would need it to be easy to enter the game. However, high barriers to entry, such as the time and cost of obtaining FDA approval, make it such that only very few can compete. That does not mean that the solution is to re-move these barriers. The FDA approval process developed from a very real danger posed by unsafe products being sold to the pub-lic under the guise of medicine—most frequently to women and children. For example, the Food Drug and Cosmetic Act which has been causing problems for "black market IUD" importing doctors came from public outcry over Elixir Sulfanilamide, a so-called "wonder-drug" that was in reality little more than an-tifreeze.[4] The elixir was marketed as a treatment for children, and caused over 100 deaths. Subsequently, the Food, Drug, and Cosmetic Act required for the first time that all drugs marketed in the US prove that a drug is safe for use before it can be sold.

The efficacy of this legislation was demonstrated in the 1960's, during the thalidomide tragedy. Originally marketed as a sleeping pill for pregnant women, thalidomide was eventually found to have caused serious birth defects including brain dam-age, blindness, deafness, and extreme deformities of the limbs. Over 10,000 children worldwide were born with thalidomide-re-lated birth defects, but because the treatment was never approved by the FDA, exposure was limited to tablets distributed to doctors on an "investigational basis," only 17 children were born with thalidomide-related deformities in the United States. At the time that thalidomide's application for drug approval was under review by the FDA, Frances Oldham Kelsey, the woman in charge of the review, earned complaints to her superiors that she was, "unreasonable and nit-picking, and that she was delaying the drug's approval unnecessarily."[5] Richardson-Merrell, the company promoting thalidomide, had been hoping to have their product approved and on the market in time for sedative season, reportedly telling Kelsey that, "We want to get this drug on the market before Christmas, because that is when our best sales are."[6] Nonetheless, Kelsey remained unconvinced of the drug's safety, a concern that became increasingly justified as European doctors began reporting a growing number of babies with abnormally short limbs, with toes sprouting directly from the hips, and flipper-like arms. Other children had been born with malformed internal organs or eye and ear defects. Additional women experienced miscarriages or gave birth to infants who died shortly after. These birth defects were later found to have been caused by thalidomide, and many countries subsequently pulled the drug from their markets—against the wishes of the producing company.

The thalidomide tragedy clearly indicates that the FDA serves an important safety function to the American people. Unfortunately, it was not until the Dalkon disaster that the FDA expanded to also require that medical devices demonstrate safety prior to entering the American market, and thousands of American women were injured by the Dalkon Shield, some to the point of death. Nonetheless, the importance of the FDA cannot credibly be in question, and as long as Americans consumers want a reasonable assurance of medicine safety, the corresponding barrier to entry it imposes will always be a regrettable but necessary impediment to high competition and low pharmaceutical prices.

But the approval process alone does not justify America's uniquely high drug prices, and not all of the FDA's efforts appear to be in the pursuit of public safety. In defense of the doctors prosecuted for the parallel imports of "black market IUDs" I argued that the circumstances indicate regulatory capture on the part of the American people, in that the FDA has at times disproportionately protected business interests over consumer welfare. It's important to remember that institutions, however necessary, are just as fallible as the people who comprise them. One wrong turn could have been in 2002 when, at the last minute, the nomination for Dr. Alistair Wood to become new commissioner of the FDA was withdrawn, reportedly due to pressures from industry:"[T]here was a great deal of concern that he [Wood] put too much emphasis on [drug] safety,"[7] explained representative Bill Frist (R-Tenn).The nomination for Wood was replaced by one for Dr. Mark McClellan, brother of then White House Press Secretary and known for his pro-business stances, such as advocating for higher pharmaceutical prices in developing nations and advocating for direct-to-consumer (DTC) advertising on the grounds that it "benefits the public health." In that respect Dr. McClellan finds himself in the minority opinion, in that as much as 80% of physicians oppose direct to consumer advertising,[8] and in fact it's illegal in most countries, with the sole exceptions of The United States and New Zealand.

For whatever reason, many mechanisms within many US institutions appear to favor business interests over the public good. At this point in time, doctors risk fines and prison time for importing cheaper drugs from Canada, even for devices which are identical those approved by the FDA for sale within the United States and pose no threat to safety. At the same time, large pharmaceutical companies have increasingly been purchasing active pharmaceutical ingredients from uninspected, unregulated offshore manufacture sites, with no subsequent prosecution when safety is breached. The public health program for America's senior citizens is legally forbidden from negotiating low prices for prescription medicines. Even the Department of Veterans Affairs is unable to obtain pharmaceuticals for prices that match those obtained in Europe, despite serving more clients. Pharmaceutical companies readily acknowledge that they prioritize profits, and the consequential skewing the direction of healthcare has been well documented. As the single largest source of pharmaceutical profits in the world, and the only significant market-based reimbursement source in the world, Americans are clearly responsible for perverting the incentives in medicine—that is, if these circumstances do indeed reflect choices made by American citizens. The degree to which Americans can be held responsible for the system as it currently stands is limited to the degree to which Americans can realistically control institutions within their country, or whether the circumstances have been designed by special interests.

In any functional democracy, a significant limitation of the choices that are made is the options that are given. For example, when he was campaigning against Mitt Romney, Barack Obama campaigned on the platform of healthcare reform and praised single-payer healthcare, implying advocacy for the system. The "ObamaCare" healthcare reform that Americans received after the election included neither a single-payer system nor the possibility for parallel imports, and was indeed very similar to the so-called "Romney Care" that his opponent had implemented as governor of Massachusetts. In this way, Americans were never offered a meaningful choice in the healthcare reform they were to receive, only who was going to give it to them.

Past the misplaced choice in the person who was to deliver the healthcare reform over the content of the reform itself, even Americans' real desires towards their healthcare are a matter of contention. Filmmaker Michael Moore came under criticism in 2009 when he claimed on Larry King Live that the majority of Americans want single-payer healthcare. Further investigation revealed that his claim was inaccurate, but not for the reasons his opponents claimed. The crux of the matter is that Americans' responses are highly dependent on the specific wording of the question. For example, when a Kaiser Permanente poll asked Americans if they were in favor of, "Having a national health plan — or single-payer plan — in which all Americans would get their insurance from a single government plan,"[9] approximately 40% favored it, and a slight majority of 50% opposed the idea. Around the same time, a CBS/New York Times poll compared results from 1979 to a 2009 poll in which Americans were asked, "Should the government in Washington provide national health insurance, or is this something that should be left only to private enterprise?"[10] When the question was framed in this way, only 32% of Americans favored private enterprise in 2009, compared to 59% favoring a government plan and 9% with no opinion. These types of conflicting opinion polls lend themselves well to cherry-picking, and has led some to believe that Americans don't know what they want, which is a highly superficial reading of the significance. The most important commonality between these polls is that the phrasing in both precluded choice. Kaiser asked if, "all Americans" should have government plans, and CBS/NYT asked if insurance should be left, "only to private enterprise," and in each poll the majority of Americans disagreed with the option that limited consumer choice. Similarly, researcher Robert Blendon reports that in 2000 when Americans were asked in general about a tax-funded health plan, 56% were in favor.[11] But when the question specified that, "all Americans would get their insurance from this plan," support for the idea dropped to only 38%. The cumulative indication is not that Americans prefer one sector over the other or don't know what they want from their healthcare system, but rather that Americans tend to bristle at words like "all" and "only", and at the thought of choices being taken away from them—which is why I find it hard to believe that a system that requires trade restrictions, prohibits price negotiation, and rewards state-enforced monopolies, actually reflects their desires, or is one that they would choose for themselves if they were empowered to do so. Quite frankly, it sounds a lot more like the kind of system private industry would design; not what American people want.

Further, in an analysis of Americans' attitudes towards health reform over the past 50 years, Blendon found that Americans' views were consistent only on a single subject: government mistrust. 1964 saw an all-time low of American mistrust in government, with only 22% of Americans reporting that they trust the government to do what is right, "only some or none of the time." Incidentally, 1964 is the last time the public has vociferously demanded that the government provide public health insurance, when 14,000 senior citizens marched at the Democratic convention in order to demand that the impending Medicaid legislation be extended to include the elderly.[12] Since 1964, mistrust in government has climbed fairly steadily, with 69% reporting mistrust in the government by 2000.

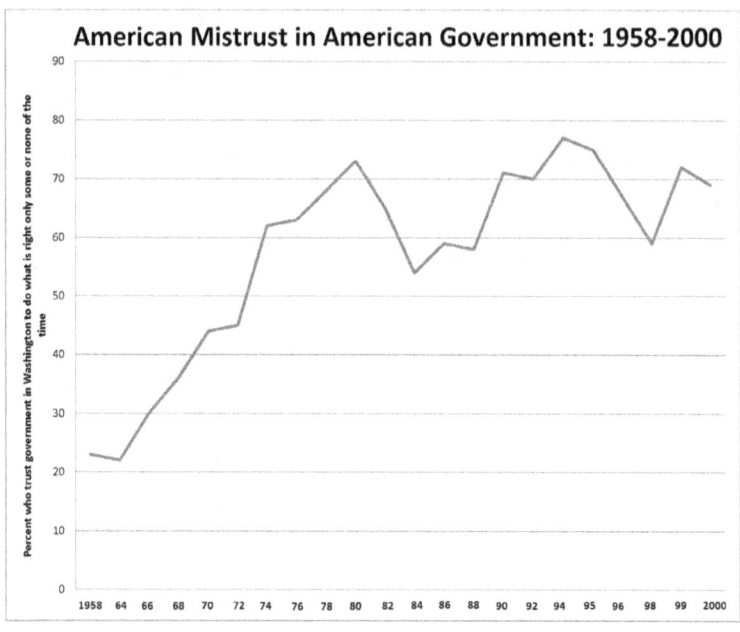

*Figure 9: Source: Blendon (2001)*

However, it's important to note that whatever thing or things the United States government has done to lose the trust of its people between the 1960's and the 2000s, mismanaging healthcare is not one of them. In his 50 year analysis Blendon also noted that in a half century's worth of healthcare reform from 1945 to 2000, Medicare is the only healthcare reform that Americans supported both before and after they received the change. Americans actually supported Medicare slightly more after receiving it than beforehand. More importantly, like the Veterans Health Administration, Medicare recipients report reasonably high levels of satisfaction to the American Consumer Satisfaction Index (ACSI). In the years in which data for Medicare recipient satisfaction was collected, Medicare recipients gave the program a satisfaction rating of between 73 and 79, with an average of score of 76 between 2001 and 2006, compared to the lower average score of 69 for the private insurance sector over the same time period. However, both of these scores are dwarfed by the Veterans Health Administration approval rating, which tends to see an approval rating in the mid-80's. Put simply—Americans who receive government provided healthcare and health insurance quite like it. Not only that, they like it more than their compatriots like their private sector equivalent.

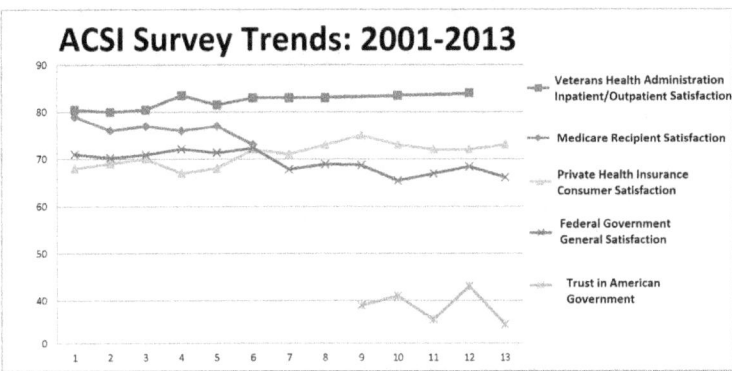

*Figure 10: Source: http://www.theacsi.org*

Additionally, not only does Americans' satisfaction with their public healthcare experience exceed their satisfaction with private health insurance, but it also exceeds their general satisfaction with the federal government—the satisfaction level for which hovered between ratings of 66 and 72. If the results of the ACSI survey can be trusted, it would be inaccurate to generalize—or dare I say, exploit—Americans' mistrust towards their federal government in general to the specific arena of healthcare. In fact, Americans continued to mistrust their government as much as ever in the post-millennial period, reporting trust levels between 35 and 43, but apparently this mistrust had no effect on their high levels of satisfaction with public health insurance (Medicare) and single-payer public healthcare (The Veterans Health Administration).

Some critics have argued that it is unfair to compare Americans' lukewarm feelings towards the private health insurance industry with the overwhelmingly positive ratings the Veterans Health Administration inpatient/outpatient services receive. After all, the VHA provides healthcare, not health insurance—so it's not exactly the same thing. This view ignores that health insurance is not a desirable end in itself but a means to an end: quality affordable healthcare. If a person is receives the ends without requiring the means that does not provide an argument against the comparison, but rather provides an argument for abolishing the means—i.e. a national dependence on private health insurance.

More recently, in 2009 Economist Ewe Reinhardt has contributed what might be the most honest argument against single-payer healthcare in America: The US is too corrupt. "When you go to Taiwan or Canada," Reinhardt said, "the kind of lobbying we have here is illegal there. You can't pay money to influence the party the same way.... Here you have basically a board of directors in the House Ways and Means Committee that gets money from lobbyists both at the regulatory writing stage and during normal operations. And they can call an administrator and demand they stop something from happening."[13]

The problem with Reinhardt's argument is that it does not address the problem. Americans may mistrust their government —for good reason, if it has been as corrupted as Reinhardt and many others charge—but knee-jerk response of running away from a corrupt government straight into the arms of the private interests that corrupted it is an illogical mass form of Stockholm Syndrome, not to mention a resignation to helplessness. Like an American illegally importing drugs from abroad, quietly ignoring the camouflaged elephant in the room, or fearing potential bias of prizes in favor of pharmaceutical perversion and de facto plutocracy—little good will come from direct refusals to confront the cause of the problem. Americans need to stop allowing complex questions to be oversimplified into false dichotomies that manipulate the answer by controlling the parameters in which the question is framed.

One additional example of a false dichotomy is the issue of public healthcare versus private industry in America. As noted, Americans tend to be opposed to any proposal that limits their choice, regardless of whether that limitation is phrased in such a way that it mandates "all Americans would get their insurance from this plan," or that insurance would be left to "only private enterprise." But there's absolutely no reason to assume that all Americans would have to agree with one of these options. As it currently stands, American healthcare comprises a three tiered spectrum of public and private integration. There are American citizens who see private healthcare providers and purchase private health insurance plans, either individually or through their place of employment. There is the public contract model utilized by Medicare and Medicaid, in which American citizens choose private healthcare providers and the service is paid for with public funds. Finally, there is also the public integration model used by the Veterans Health Administration, in which American citizens receive healthcare from a public hospital that is funded by public dollars. As it is, three variations of public and private integration coexist within the United States healthcare system, and there is absolutely no honest reason to imply that expanding any one of these options would necessitate eliminating either of the other two, any more than providing clean drinking water to the public inevitably dismantles the bottled water industry, or a public police force replaces the private security industry. Americans shouldn't be asked to restrict what option is available to all Americans, only what's best for them as individuals.

The specific case study of the intrauterine device does not on its own support conclusions regarding the broader failing of the pharmaceutical market, regulatory capture, or even public discourse in America. The purpose of this book was to investigate one microcosmic aspect so thoroughly that other, related subjects may eventually be credibly broached. The pricing mechanisms of IUDs and their related issues represent initial stages of broader inquiry into subject of healthcare rationing in America, the rationale behind various pharmaceutical pricing systems and their consequences, the real effects of intellectual property enforcement, which includes prosecuting doctors and withholding medicine from the ill and impoverished, and much more. The real conclusion is: American medicine is sick, it will not be healed by the forces that corrupted it, and in order to begin the process Americans will first need to start asking a lot more of their own stupid questions.

# NOTES

[1]     Pritchett (2006)

[2]     Samuelson (2009)

[3]     In this point I'm paraphrasing Chris Hedges, who wrote, "A democratic state begins from the assumption that most of those who gravitate toward power are mediocre and probably immoral. It assumes that we must always protect ourselves from bad government. We must be prepared for the worst leaders even as we hope for the best. And as Karl Popper wrote, this understanding leads to a new approach to power, for 'it forces us to replace the question: Who shall rule? By the new question: How can we so organize political institutions that bad or incompetent rulers can be prevented from doing too much damage?'" See Hedges (2008).

[4]     FDA History Part III: Drugs and Foods Under the 1938 Act and Its Amendments (2009)

[5]     Bren (2001)

[6]     Bren (2001)

[7]     Quoted in Wei (2007)

[8]     Norris (2005) pg 17

[9]      Politicofact.com (2009)

[10]     CBS/NYT (2009)

[11]     Blendon (2000)

[12]     Hoffman (2003)

[13]     Quoted in Klein (2014)

# Appendix A

**Contraception use, induced abortions, unintended & unwanted births:
1982-2010**

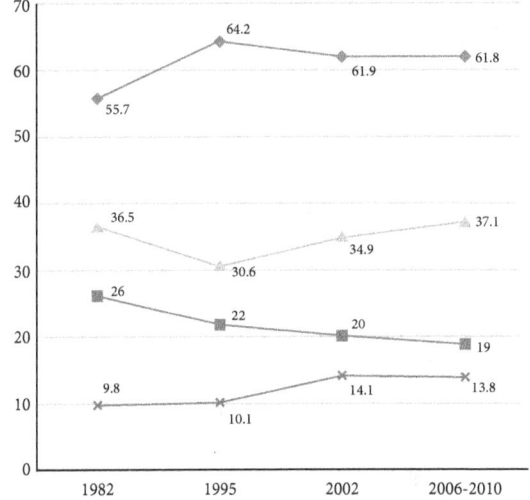

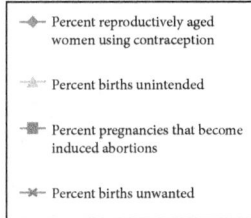

| | Number in thousands[a] | | | |
|---|---|---|---|---|
| Year | Total Pregnancies | Total live births | Total induced abortions | Total fetal losses |
| 1976 | 5002 | 3168 | 1179 | 655 |
| 1977 | 5331 | 3327 | 1317 | 687 |
| 1978 | 5433 | 3333 | 1410 | 690 |
| 1979 | 5714 | 3494 | 1498 | 722 |
| 1980 | 5912 | 3612 | 1554 | 746 |
| 1981 | 5958 | 3629 | 1577 | 751 |
| 1982 | 6024 | 3681 | 1574 | 769 |
| 1983 | 5977 | 3639 | 1575 | 763 |
| 1984 | 6019 | 3669 | 1577 | 773 |
| 1985 | 6144 | 3761 | 1589 | 795 |
| 1986 | 6129 | 3757 | 1574 | 798 |
| 1987 | 6183 | 3809 | 1559 | 815 |
| 1988 | 6393 | 3910 | 1591 | 893 |
| 1989 | 6527 | 4041 | 1567 | 919 |
| 1990 | 6786 | 4158 | 1609 | 1019 |
| 1991 | 6682 | 4111 | 1557 | 1014 |
| 1992 | 6603 | 4065 | 1529 | 1009 |
| 1993 | 6494 | 4000 | 1495 | 999 |
| 1994 | 6370 | 3953 | 1423 | 994 |
| 1995 | 6245 | 3900 | 1359 | 986 |
| 1996 | 6240 | 3891 | 1360 | 988 |
| 1997 | 6205 | 3881 | 1335 | 989 |
| 1998 | 6266 | 3942 | 1319 | 1006 |
| 1999 | 6286 | 3959 | 1315 | 1011 |
| 2000 | 6438 | 4059 | 1313 | 1066 |
| 2001 | 6374 | 4026 | 1291 | 1057 |
| 2002 | 6347 | 4022 | 1269 | 1056 |
| 2003 | 6415 | 4090 | 1250 | 1075 |
| 2004 | 6450 | 4112 | 1222 | 1090 |
| 2005 | 6435 | 4138 | 1206 | 1091 |
| 2006 | 6632 | 4266 | 1242 | 1124 |
| 2007 | 6663 | 4316 | 1210 | 1137 |
| 2008 | 6578 | 4248 | 1212 | 1118 |

| Year | Percent* | | |
|---|---|---|---|
| | Percent pregnancies become live births | Percent pregnancies become induced abortions | Percent pregnancies become fetal losses |
| 1976 | 63.33 | 23.57 | 13.09 |
| 1977 | 62.40 | 24.70 | 12.88 |
| 1978 | 61.34 | 25.95 | 12.70 |
| 1979 | 61.14 | 26.21 | 12.63 |
| 1980 | 61.09 | 26.28 | 12.61 |
| 1981 | 60.90 | 26.46 | 12.60 |
| 1982 | 61.11 | 26.13 | 12.77 |
| 1983 | 60.88 | 26.35 | 12.77 |
| 1984 | 60.96 | 26.20 | 12.84 |
| 1985 | 61.21 | 25.86 | 12.94 |
| 1986 | 61.30 | 25.68 | 13.02 |
| 1987 | 61.60 | 25.21 | 13.18 |
| 1988 | 61.16 | 24.89 | 13.97 |
| 1989 | 61.91 | 24.01 | 14.08 |
| 1990 | 61.27 | 23.71 | 15.02 |
| 1991 | 61.52 | 23.30 | 15.18 |
| 1992 | 61.56 | 23.16 | 15.28 |
| 1993 | 61.60 | 23.02 | 15.38 |
| 1994 | 62.06 | 22.34 | 15.60 |
| 1995 | 62.45 | 21.76 | 15.79 |
| 1996 | 62.36 | 21.79 | 15.83 |
| 1997 | 62.55 | 21.51 | 15.94 |
| 1998 | 62.91 | 21.05 | 16.05 |
| 1999 | 62.98 | 20.92 | 16.08 |
| 2000 | 63.05 | 20.39 | 16.56 |
| 2001 | 61.16 | 20.25 | 16.58 |
| 2002 | 63.37 | 19.99 | 16.64 |
| 2003 | 63.76 | 19.49 | 16.76 |
| 2004 | 63.75 | 18.95 | 16.90 |
| 2005 | 64.30 | 18.74 | 16.95 |
| 2006 | 63.32 | 18.73 | 16.95 |
| 2007 | 64.78 | 18.16 | 17.06 |
| 2008 | 64.58 | 18.43 | 17.00 |

*Percentages are author's calculations from cited data source.

| | Number in thousands | | | |
|---|---|---|---|---|
| | Number women ages 15-44[b] | Total pregnancies[a] | Total live births[a] | Total abortions[a] |
| 1982 | 54,099 | 6,024 | 3,681 | 1,574 |
| 1995 | 60,201 | 6,245 | 3,900 | 1,359 |
| 2002 | 61,651 | 6,347 | 4,022 | 1,269 |
| 2006-2010 | 61,864*** | 6,632** | 4,266** | 1,242** |
| | Percent | | | |
| | Percent women using contraception, ages 15-44b | Percent births unintendedc | Percent births unwantedc | Percent pregnancies became induced abortions* |
| 1982 | 55.7 | 36.5% | 9.8% | 26.12% |
| 1995 | 64.1 | 30.6% | 10.1% | 21.76% |
| 2002 | 61.9 | 34.9% | 14.1% | 19.99% |
| 2006-2010 | 61.8*** | 37.1%*** | 13.8%*** | 18.72%** |

*Percentages are author's calculations from cited data source.

**Number applicable to 2006 only

***Number applicable to period between 2006-2010

**Sources:**

[a]Ventura, Stephanie J., et al. "Estimated pregnancy rates and rates of pregnancy outcomes for the United States, 1990-2008." National vital statistics reports: from the Centers for Disease Control and Prevention, National Center for Health Statistics, National Vital Statistics System 60.7 (2012): 1.

[b]Mosher, William D., and Jo Jones. "Use of contraception in the United States: 1982-2008." Vital and health statistics. Series 23, Data from the National Survey of Family Growth 29 (2010): 1.

[c]Mosher, William D., Jo Jones, and Joyce C. Abma. Intended and unintended births in the United States: 1982-2010. US Department of Health and Human Services, Centers for Disease Control and Prevention, National Center for Health Statistics, 2012.

# APPENDIX B

Due to the, "shroud of secrecy draped over the health care prices" (Reinhardt 2013) and consequential difficulty of obtaining pharmaceutical pricing data, all prices collected from publicly published resources, and PPP adjusted according to World bank PPP adjustment chart:

http://data.worldbank.org/indicator/PA.NUS.PPPC.RF

| Year | Country | Sector | Device price in USD | PPP adjusted, respective year | Adjusted for inflation to 2013 US dollars1 | PPP and inflation adjusted for 2013 | GDP per capita, respective year[2] | Source |
|------|---------|--------|---------------------|-------------------------------|--------------------------------------------|-------------------------------------|-----------------------------------|--------|
| 1987 | USA | Unspecified | $25 | - | $51.29 | - | 20,101 | Ramirez (1987) |
| 1991 | USA | Private AWP | $184 | - | $314.71 | - | 24,405 | Trussell et al. (1995, 1997a) |
| 1993 | USA | Public (Medi-Cal) | $109 | - | $175.73 | - | 26,465 | Trussell et al. (1995, 1997a) |
| 1998 | Egypt | Public | $1.46 | $3.65 | $2.09 | $5.22 | 3,356 | Moreland (2000) |
| 1999-2003 | Russia | Unspecified | $11 imported | $39.29 | 14.47 | $51.68 | 7,485 | David et al. (2007) |
| 2000 | International Public Procurement | Public | $0.49 | - | $0.66 | - | - | Green (2002) |
| 2001 | USA | Private AWP | $358.80 | - | $471.96 | - | 37,286 | Chiou (2003) |
| 2001 | UK | Public (British National Formulary) | $13.16 | $14.62 | $17.32 | $19.23 | 27,853 | Dennis et al. (2002) |

| Year | Country | Sector | Device price in USD | PPP adjusted, respective year | Adjusted for inflation to 2013 US dollars1 | PPP and inflation adjusted for 2013 | GDP per capita, respective year[2] | Source |
|------|---------|--------|------|------|------|------|------|--------|
| 2002 | USA | Public | $164 | - | $212.37 | - | 38,175 | Rodriguez et al. (2010) |
| 2005 | Bolivia | Non profit CIF** | $1.95 | $6.50 | $2.33 | $7.75 | 3,688 | Sarley et al. (2006) |
| 2005 | Bolivia | Public CIF** | $0.35 | $1.16 | 0.42 | $1.38 | 3,688 | Sarley et al. (2006) |
| 2005 | Brazil | Public CIF** | $3.20 | $5.33 | 3.82 | $6.36 | 8,502 | Sarley et al. (2006) |
| 2005 | Chile | Public CIF** | $0.31 | $0.51 | 0.37 | $0.61 | 12,773 | Sarley et al. (2006) |
| 2005 | Chile | Non profit CIF** | $0.81 | $1.35 | 0.97 | $1.61 | 12,773 | Sarley et al. (2006) |
| 2005 | Ecuador | Public CIF** | $2.89 | $7.22 | 3.45 | $8.61 | 7,129 | Sarley et al. (2006) |
| 2005 | Paraguay | Non profit CIF** | $0.56 | $1.60 | 0.67 | $1.91 | 4,554 | Sarley et al. (2006) |
| 2005 | Paraguay | Public CIF** | $0.42 | $1.20 | 0.50 | $1.43 | 4,554 | Sarley et al. (2006) |
| 2005 | Peru | Public CIF** | $0.54 | $1.08 | 0.64 | $1.29 | 6,349 | Sarley et al. (2006) |
| 2005 | Dominican Republic | Non profit CIF** | $0.75 | $1.36 | 0.89 | $1.62 | 6,326 | Sarley et al. (2006) |
| 2005 | Dominican Republic | Public CIF** | $0.33 | $0.60 | 0.39 | $0.72 | 6,326 | Sarley et al. (2006) |
| 2005 | Guatemala | Non profit CIF** | $1.57 | $3.14 | 1.87 | $3.75 | 4,074 | Sarley et al. (2006) |
| 2005 | Guatemala | Public CIF** | $1.49 | $2.98 | 1.78 | $3.55 | 4,074 | Sarley et al. (2006) |
| 2005 | Nicaragua | Public CIF** | $1.63 | $4.08 | 1.94 | $4.87 | 3,013 | Sarley et al. (2006) |
| 2006 | China | Public | $0.32 | $0.80 | $0.37 | $0.92 | 4,753 | Wen et al. (2010) |
| 2007 | USA | Private AWP -15% | $494 | - | $555.03 | - | 48,070 | Trussell (2009) |

| Year | Country | Sector | Device price in USD | PPP adjusted, respective year | Adjusted for inflation to 2013 US dollars1 | PPP and inflation adjusted for 2013 | GDP per capita, respective year[2] | Source |
|------|---------|--------|---------|---------|---------|---------|---------|--------|
| 2008 | Canada | Unspec-ified | $72.13 | $60.11 | $78.08 | $65.04 | 38,987 | Stubbs et al. (2008) |
| 2012 | USA | Private AWP | $718 | - | $728.87 | - | 51,749 | Trussell (2012) |
| 2012 | USA | Private | $598 | - | $606.76 | - . | 51,749 | Trussell et al. (2013) |
| 2013 | Inter-na-tional Public Pro-cure-ment | Public | $0.50-$1.50 | - | - | - | - | PATH (2013) |

* **AWP:** Average Wholesale Price. It should be noted that the "Average Wholesale Price" is a misnomer, dubbed "Ain't What's Paid," by Berndt (2010), in that it's well known within the medical industry that real prices are usually approximately 15% below the AWP. However, the AWP cannot be dismissed out of hand, as it is nonetheless used as a standard benchmark, including in the determination of public reimbursement amounts.

**\*\*CIF:** Cost insurance freight (CIF) is the cost of the commodity, including the cost of insurance and transport to the port of destination or entry. This is fairly comparable to the ex-manufacturer, or Average Manufacturer Price (AMP) and Average Wholesale Price (AWP).

## References:

[1]US Department of Labor. Bureau Labor Statistics: CPI Inflation Calculator. Web accessed Dec 11 2013 from: http://www.bls.gov/data/inflation_calculator.htm

[2]World Bank, International Comparison Program Database. Web accessed Dec 11 2013 from: http://data.worldbank.org/indicator/NY.GDP.PCAP.PP.CD

# APPENDIX C

**Public and Private Sector ParaGard & Mirena Price Increase:**
**1991 to 2012**

all prices controlled for inflation, converted to 2013 US dollars

| Year | ParaGard Public Sector Price | | ParaGard Private Sector Price | | Mirena Private Sector Price | | Source |
|---|---|---|---|---|---|---|---|
| | As listed | Con-verted to 2013 Dollars | As listed | Con-verted to 2013 Dollars | As listed | Con-verted to 2013 Dollars | |
| 1991 | - | - | 184 | 314.71 | - | - | Trussell et al. (1995, 1997a) |
| 1993 | 109 | 175.73 | - | - | - | - | Trussell et al. (1995, 1997a) |
| 2001 | - | - | 358.80 | 471.96 | 395 | 519.58 | Chiou (2003) |
| 2002 | 164 | 212.37 | - | - | - | - | Rodriguez et al. (2010) |
| 2007 | - | - | 581.17* | 652.97 | 689.25* | 774.40 | Trussell (2009) |
| 2008 | 588.98 | 637.27 | - | - | - | - | FSS** |
| 2012 | - | - | 718 | 728.87 | 844 | 855.35 | Trussell (2012) |

*Research paper indicates that price cited is Average Wholesale Price (AWP) minus 15%. For consistency in cross comparability, price was converted back to AWP.

** Federal Supply Schedule searchable from:

http://www.va.gov/nac/index.cfm?template=Search_Pharmaceutical_Catalog

# APPENDIX D

**ASCI Survey Trends: 2001-2013**

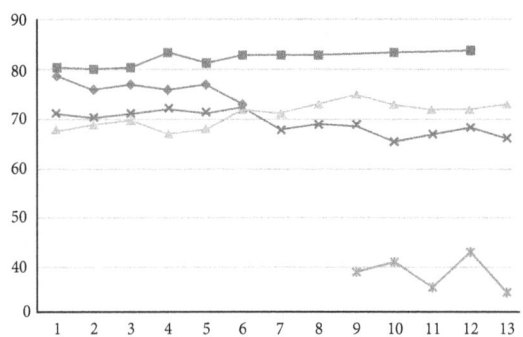

Legend:
- Veterans Health Administration Inpatient/Outpatient Satisfaction
- Medicare Recipient Satisfaction
- Private Health Insurance Consumer Satisfaction
- Federal Government General Satisfaction
- Trust in American Government

| ASCI Annual Consumer Satisfaction Ratings: 2001-2013 | | | | | |
|---|---|---|---|---|---|
| Year | Veterans Health Administration Inpatient/ Outpatient Satisfaction* | Medicare Recipient Satisfaction | Private Health Insurance Consumer Satisfaction | Federal Government General Satisfaction | Trust in American Government |
| 2001 | 80.5 | 79 | 68 | 71 | NA** |
| 2002 | 80 | 76 | 69 | 70.2 | NA** |
| 2003 | 80.5 | 77 | 70 | 70.9 | NA** |
| 2004 | 83.5 | 76 | 67 | 72.1 | NA** |
| 2005 | 81.5 | 77 | 68 | 71.3 | NA** |
| 2006 | 83 | 73 | 72 | 72.3 | NA** |
| 2007 | 82.5 | NA** | 71 | 67.8 | NA** |
| 2008 | 83 | NA** | 73 | 68.9 | NA** |
| 2009 | NA** | NA** | 75 | 68.7 | 39 |
| 2010 | 83.5 | NA** | 73 | 65.4 | 41 |
| 2011 | NA** | NA** | 72 | 66.9 | 36 |
| 2012 | 84 | NA** | 72 | 68.4 | 43 |
| 2013 | NA** | NA** | 73 | 66.1 | 35 |

*VHA Inpatient/Outpatient scores averaged to get aggregate satisfaction score

**Information either not measured that year or otherwise not available.

# REFERENCES

A Brief History: Universal Health Care Efforts in the US. Physicians for a National Health Program. Web accessed February 1st 2014 from: http://www.pnhp.org/facts/a-brief-history-universal-health-care-efforts-in-the-us

Aaron, H.J. "The Cost of Health Care Administration in the United States and Canada—Questionable Answers to a Questionable Question," New England Journal of Medicine 349, no. 8 (2003): 801–303.

American College of Obstetricians and Gynecologists (ACOG). Adolescents and long-acting reversible contraception: implants and intra-uterine devices. Committee Opinion No. 539. Obstet Gynecol 2012; 120:983-8.

Anderson, Gerard F., et al. "It's the prices, stupid: why the United States is so different from other countries." Health Affairs 22.3 (2003): 89-105.

Anderson, Gerard F., et al. "Doughnut holes and price controls." Health Affairs 21 (2004).

Angell, Marcia. The truth about the drug companies: How they deceive us and what to do about it. Random House LLC, 2005.

Ashford, Lori, Jay Gribble, and Donna Clifton. Family planning saves lives. Washington DC: Population Reference Bureau, 2009.

Bailey, Martha J. "More power to the pill: the impact of contraceptive freedom on women's life cycle labor supply." The Quarterly Journal of Economics 121.1 (2006): 289-320.

Bailey, Martha J., Brad Hershbein, and Amalia R. Miller. The opt-in revolution? Contraception and the gender gap in wages. No. w17922. National Bureau of Economic Research, 2012.

Baker, Dean. "Financing drug research: What are the issues?." 2008 Industry Studies Conference Paper. 2008.

Barot, Sneha. "In Search of Breakthroughs: Renewing Support for Contraceptive Research and Development." Guttmacher Policy Review 16.1 (2013).

Bayer Annual Report 2009. Available at: http://www.annualreport2009.bayer.com/en/Combined-Management-Report-BayerGroup-Bayer-AG-2009.pdfx. Accessed December 5, 2013.

Beer, K., et al. "Assessment of India's locally manufactured contraceptive product supply." Lancet Infectious Diseases 6.9 (2006): 544.

Belden, Peter, Cynthia C. Harper, and J. Joseph Speidel. "The copper IUD for emergency contraception, a neglected option." Contraception 85.4 (2012): 338-339.

Berndt, Ernst R., and Joseph P. Newhouse. Pricing and reimbursement in US pharmaceutical markets. No. w16297. National Bureau of Economic Research, 2010.

Bhosle, Monali J., and Rajesh Balkrishnan. "Drug reimportation practices in the United States." Therapeutics and clinical risk management 3.1 (2007): 41.

Black, Kirsten, and Ali Kubba. "Non-hormonal contraception."

Obstetrics, Gynaecology & Reproductive Medicine 21.4 (2011): 103-106.

Blendon, Robert J., and John M. Benson. "Americans' views on health policy: a fifty-year historical perspective." Health Affairs 20.2 (2001): 33-46.

Blumenthal, P. D., A. Voedisch, and K. Gemzell-Danielsson. "Strategies to prevent unintended pregnancy: increasing use of long-acting reversible contraception." Human reproduction update 17.1 (2011): 121-137.

Boldrin, Michele, and David K. Levine. Against Intellectual Monopoly. Cambridge: Cambridge University Press, 2008.

Bren, Linda. Frances Oldham Kelsey: FDA Medical Reviewer Leaves Her Mark on History. FDA Consumer magazine. Published March-April 2001. Accessed March 12 2014 from: http://permanent.access.gpo.gov/lps1609/www.fda.gov/fdac/features/2001/201_kelsey.html

Brown SS and Eisenberg LE, eds., The Best Intentions: Unintended Pregnancy and the Well-Being of Children and Families, Washington, DC: National Academy Press, 1995.

Bullough, Vern L., ed. Encyclopedia of birth control. ABC-CLIO, 2001.

Carey, et al. Health care reform in the United States. OECD working Paper, 2009.

CBS/NYT Poll: American public opinion: Today vs. 30 Years ago. Publicly released February 1, 2009.

Centers for Disease Control and Prevention. Ten Great Public Health Achievements in the 20th Century: 1900-1999. Web accessed January 28 2014 from http://www.cdc.gov/about/history/tengpha.htm

Chandrasekaran, N., and S. Mohan Kumar. Pharmaceutical Supply Chain Challenges and Best Practices. Vol. 20. working paper, 2003.

Chiou, Chiun-Fang, et al. "Economic analysis of contraceptives for women." Contraception 68.1 (2003): 3-10.

Chirina, Svetlana, et al. "Satisfaction, Early Removal, and Side Effects Associated With Long-Acting Reversible Contraception." Family medicine 45.10 (2013): 701-7.

Clifton D, Kaneda T, Ashford L. Family Planning Worldwide 2008 Data Sheet. Washington, DC: Population Reference Bureau; 2008.

Congressional Budget Office. Research and development in the pharmaceutical industry. Washington, DC: Congress of the United States, October 2006.

Contraceptive Technology Update. More women are looking at intrauterine devices. 2004 Nov; 25(11)

Couzin-Frankel, Jennifer. Contraceptive Comeback: The Maligned IUD Gets a Second Chance. Wired Magazine. Published July 15, 2011. Web accessed Dec 11 2013 from: http://www.wired.com/magazine/2011/07/ff_iud/all/

Creese, et al. World Medicine Situation. World Health Organization (WHO); 2004. Report no: WHO/EDM/PAR/2004.5

Crosignani, P. G. "Intrauterine devices and intrauterine systems." Human Reproduction Update. 14.3 (2008): 197-208.

Cruz v. Whitney. Medical Board of California Department of Consumer Affairs. Case Number 06-2009-200309. (2012) Web accessed 11 Dec 2013 from: http://www.healthgrades.com/media/english/pdf/sanctions/HGPYAC872ECE85919751707032012.pdf

Daemmrich, Arthur A. US Healthcare Reform and the Pharmaceutical Industry. Harvard Business School, 2011.

Daniels, Norman, Brendan Saloner, and Adriane H. Gelpi. "Access, cost, and financing: achieving an ethical health reform." Health Affairs 28.5 (2009): w909-w916

Danzon P.M. and M.F. Furukawa (2003). Prices and availability of pharmaceuticals: Evidence from nine countries. Health Affairs. web exclusive, pp. W3.521-536.

David, P. H., et al. "Women's reproductive health needs in Russia: what can we learn from an intervention to improve post-abortion care?." Health Policy and planning 22.2 (2007): 83-94.

Dayen , David. Dorgan Amendment Slashed After Last-Minute PhRMa Deal PhRMa Hasn't Agreed To. Firedoglake. Published December 16, 2009. Web accessed April 11, 2015 from: http://news.firedoglake.com/2009/12/16/dorgan-amendment-slashed-after-last-minute-phrma-deal-phrma-hasnt-agreed-to/

DeNavas-Walt, Carmen, Bernadette D. Proctor, and Jessica C. Smith. US Census Bureau, Current Population Reports, P60-245, Income, Poverty, and Health Insurance Coverage in the United States: 2012, US Government Printing Office, Washington, DC, 2013.

Dennis, Jo, and Naomi Hampton. "IUDs: which device?." Journal of Family Planning and Reproductive Health Care 28.2 (2002): 61-68.

Department of Veteran Affairs. VA History in Brief. Web accessed February 2nd 2014 from: http://www.va.gov/opa/publications/archives/docs/history_in_brief.pdf

Dickerson, Karma. Ky. doctor accused of giving women non-FDA approved birth control. Whs11.com. Published March 21,

2013. Web accessed dec 11 2013 from: http://www.whas11.com/news/health/Ky-doctor-accused-of-giving-women-non-FDA-approved-birth-control-199436601.html

DiMasi, Joseph A., Ronald W. Hansen, and Henry G. Grabowski. "The price of innovation: new estimates of drug development costs." Journal of health economics 22.2 (2003): 151-185.

Docteur, E. and H. Oxley (2003), "Health-Care Systems: Lessons from the Reform Experience", OECD Health Working Papers, No. 9, OECD Publishing. http://dx.doi.org/10.1787/865047648066

Docteur, et al. Pharmaceutical pricing policies in a global market. OECD, 2008.

Farwell, Jackie. Judge overturns Maine law allowing prescription drug imports. Bandor Daily News. Published Feb. 24, 2015. Web accessed April 11 2015 from: http://bangordailynews.com/2015/02/24/health/judge-overturns-maine-law-allowing-prescription-drug-imports/

FDA Consumer Health Information. FDA Cautions Against Using Unapproved IUDs. May 22, 2008. Web accessed Dec 11 2013 from: http://www.fda.gov/downloads/ForConsumers/ConsumerUpdates/UCM220033.pdf

FDA History Part III: Drugs and Foods Under the 1938 Act and Its Amendments. Last updated June 18 2009. Accessed March 12th 2014 form: http://www.fda.gov/AboutFDA/WhatWeDo/History/Origin/ucm055118.htm

Feldblum, et al. Randomized assignment to copper IUD or depot medroxy-progesterone acetate: feasibility of enrolment, continuation and disease ascertainment. Contraception 2005;72:187–191.

Finer, Lawrence B., Jenna Jerman, and Megan L. Kavanaugh. "Changes in use of long-acting contraceptive methods in the United States, 2007–2009." Fertility and sterility (2012).

Flynn, A. (2013). "The Title X Factor: Why the Health of America's Women Depends on More Funding for Family Planning." The Roosevelt Institute. Available from: http:// www.rooseveltinstitute.org/

Ford, Kathleen. Use of intrauterine contraceptive devices in the United States. US Department of Health, Education, and Welfare, Public Health Service, Office of the Assistant Secretary for Health, National Center for Health Statistics, 1978.

Forrest, Jacqueline Darroch. "The end of IUD marketing in the United States: What does it mean for American women?." Family planning perspectives 18.2 (1986): 52-57.

Foster, Diana Greene, et al. "Cost savings from the provision of specific methods of contraception in a publicly funded program." Journal Information 99.3 (2009).

Frank, Richard G. and Joseph P. Newhouse [2008], "Should Drug Prices Be Negotiated Under Part D of Medicare? And If So, How?", Health Affairs 27(1):33-43, January/February.

Frost, et al. The impact of publicly funded family planning clinic services on unintended pregnancies and government cost savings. Journal of Health Care for the Poor and Underserved 19.3 (2008a): 778-796.

Frost, et al. Factors associated with contraceptive choice and inconsistent method use, United States, 2004, Perspectives on Sexual and Reproductive Health, (2008b) 40(2):94–104.

Frost, Jennifer J., Stanley K. Henshaw, and Adam Sonfield."Contraceptive Needs and Services, National and

State Data, 2008 Update." (2010). Web accessed Dec 11 2013 from: http://www.guttmacher.org/pubs/win/contraceptive-needs-2008.pdf

Frost, Jennifer J., and Laura Duberstein Lindberg."Reasons for using contraception: perspectives of US women seeking care at specialized family planning clinics." Contraception (2012).

Gaffney, Alexander. Senator Looks to Spur Development of Medicines Through 'Prize Fund'. Regulatory Focus. Published May 15, 2012. Accessed March 3rd 2014 from: http://www.raps.org/focus-online/news/news-article-view/article/1508/senator-looks-to-spur-development-of-medicines-through-prize-fund.aspx

Gariepy, Aileen M., et al. "The impact of out-of-pocket expense on IUD utilization among women with private insurance." Contraception 84.6 (2011): e39-e42.

Gerth, Jeff, and Gay Stolberg, Sheryl. Drug Companies Profit From Research Supported by Taxpayers. The New York Times. Published April 23, 2000. Web accessed December 20th 2013 from: http://www.nytimes.com/library/national/science/health/042300hth-drugs.html

Gilens, Martin, and Benjamin I. Page. "Testing theories of American politics: Elites, interest groups, and average citizens." Perspectives on Politics (2014).

Gokhale, Ketaki. Merck to Bristol-Myers Face More Threats on India Patents. Bloomberg News. Published Jan 28 2014, accessed Feb 28 2014 from: http://www.bloomberg.com/news/2014-01-21/merck-to-bristol-myers-face-more-threats-on-india-patents.html

Gold, Rachel Benson. "The need for and cost of mandating private insurance coverage of contraception." Guttmacher Report on Public Policy 1.4 (1998).

Goldacre, Ben. Bad Pharma: how drug companies mislead doctors and harm patients. Random House Digital, Inc., 2013.

Goldin C, Katz L. The power of the pill: oral contraceptives and women's career and marriage decisions. J Polit Econ 2002;110:730-70.

Green, R. "Empty pockets: Estimating ability to pay for family planning." Bay area international group. Berkeley. Berkeley: University of California (2002).

Grim, Ryan. Doughnuts For Dorgan: Drug Reimportation Killed In Deal That Might Get Cheaper Drugs For Seniors. The Huffington Post. Published March 18, 2010. Web accessed April 11 2015 from: http://www.huffingtonpost.com/2009/12/15/doughnuts-for-dorgan-drug_n_393527.html

Guttmacher Institute. Testimony Submitted to the Committee on Preventive Services for Women Institute of Medicine. January 12, 2011.

Guttmacher Institute, Facts on unintended pregnancy in the United States, In Brief, (2013a),accessed Dec 20 2013, from: http://www.guttmacher.org/pubs/FBUnintended-Pregnancy-US.html.

Guttmacher Institute , Contraceptive Use in the United States. Fact Sheet, (2013b), accessed Dec 20, 2013, from: http://www.guttmacher.org.

Guttmacher Institute, Publicly Funded Contraceptive Services In The United States, Fact Sheet. (2013c). Web accessed Dec 20, 2013, from: www.guttmacher.org/pubs/FB-Costs-Benefits-Contraceptives.html

Hale, Victoria G., Katherine Woo, and Helene Levens Lipton. "Oxymoron no more: the potential of nonprofit drug companies to deliver on the promise of medicines for the developing world." Health Affairs 24.4 (2005): 1057-1063.

Hanson, Kara, Lilani Kumaranayake, and Ian Thomas. "Ends versus means: the role of markets in expanding access to contraceptives." Health Policy and Planning 16.2 (2001): 125-136.

Hard pills to swallow: Drug firms have new medicines and patients are desperate for them. But the arguments over cost are growing. The Economist print edition. Published Jan 4th 2014. Web accessed Janaury 29 2014 from: http:// www.economist.com/ news/international/21592655-drug-firms-have-new-medicines-and-patients-are-desperate-them-arguments-over

Harvey, Philip D. Let every child be wanted: How social marketing is revolutionizing contraceptive use around the world. Westport, CT: Auburn House, 1999.

Harper, Cynthia C., et al. "Challenges in translating evidence to practice: the provision of intrauterine contraception." Obstetrics & Gynecology 111.6 (2008): 1359-1369.

Hatcher RA. Contraceptive Technology. 19th rev. ed. New York: Ardent Media; 2007.

Health Care Renewal. Prosecuting Doctors for Importing IUDs from Canada, but Still No Penalties for Selling Adulterated Heparin from China. Posted July 19, 2010. Accessed Janury 20 2014 from: http://hcrenewal.blogspot.com/2010/07/prosecuting-doctors-for-importing-iuds.html

Hedges, Chris. I don't believe in atheists. New York: Continuum, 2008.

Hemel, Daniel J., and Lisa Larrimore Ouellette. "Beyond the Patents--Prizes Debate." Texas Law Review 92.2 (2013).

Hemphill, Thomas. Prescription Drug Imports: Maine Leads, the Nation Follows? American Action Forum. Published November 12, 2013. Web accessed April 11, 2015 from: http://americanaction-forum.org/insights/prescription-drug-imports-maine-leads-the-nation-follows

Herald-Leader Staff Report. Grayson County doctor gets probation for 'misbranding' of birth-control device. Kentucky.com. Published August 12, 2013. Web accessed Dec 11, 2013 from: http://www.kentucky.com/2013/08/12/2762960/grayson-county-doctor-gets-probation.html

Herper, Matthew. How To Charge $1.6 Million For a New Drug And Get Away With It. Forbes Magazine. Published March 19 2012, accessed Feb 28 2014 from: http://www.forbes.com/sites/matthewherper/2012/03/19/how-to-charge-1-6-million-for-a-new-drug-and-get-away-with-it/

HNN's History of Healthcare Reform. George Mason University History News Network. Web accessed February 11th 2014 from: http://hnn.us/article/146911

Hodges, B. 1995. Interactions with the pharmaceutical industry: Experiences and attitudes of psychiatry residents, interns and clerks. Canadian Medical Association Journal 153:553–59.

Hoffman, Beatrix. "Health care reform and social movements in the United States." American Journal of Public Health 93.1 (2003): 75-85.

How the Medicaid rebate on prescription drugs affects pricing in the pharmaceutical industry. Washington, D.C.: Congressional Budget Office, January 1996:28.

Hubacher, David. "The checkered history and bright future of intrauterine contraception in the United States." Perspectives on sexual and reproductive health 34.2 (2002): 98-103.

Hubacher, David, Lawrence B. Finer, and Eve Espey. "Renewed interest in intrauterine contraception in the United States: evidence and explanation." Contraception 83.4 (2011): 291-294.

IMAP. Pharma and Biotec Global Industry Report 2011. www.IMAP.com

Institute of Medicine (US). Initial national priorities for comparative effectiveness research. Washington, DC: National Academic Press; 2009.

IUD Malpractice Fears Exaggerated, but Cost a Concern for Patients. The Contraception Report, November 1998. Volume 9 Issue 5.

Jensen, Kristin. Vets Loving Socialized Medicine Show Government Offers Savings. Bloomberg. Published Oct 2nd, 2009. Accessed March 7th 2014 from: http://www.bloomberg.com/apps/news?pid=newsarchive&sid= aLIc5ABThjBk

Jones, Rachel K., Lawrence B. Finer, and Susheela Singh. "Characteristics of US abortion patients, 2008." New York: Guttmacher Institute (2010).

Jones, Jo, W. D. Mosher, and Kimberly Daniels. "Current contraceptive use in the United States, 2006–2010, and changes in patterns of use since 1995." Natl Vital Stat Rep 60 (2012).

Kadushin, Ronen. Bearina IUD Concept. Ronen Kadushin.com. Web accessed Dec 26 2013 from http://www.ronen-kadushin.com/index.php/open-design/bearina-iud-concept/

Kaneshiro, Bliss, and Tod Aeby. "Long-term safety, efficacy, and patient acceptability of the intrauterine Copper T-380A contraceptive device." International journal of women's health 2 (2010): 211.

Katz, Dana, Arthur L. Caplan, and Jon F. Merz. "All gifts large and small." American Journal of Bioethics 3.3 (2003): 39-46.

Klein, Ezra. Is the US too corrupt for single-payer health care? The Washington Post. Published Janaury 16th 2014. Accessed March 12 2014 from: http://www.washingtonpost.com/blogs/wonkblog/wp/2014/01/16/is-the-u-s-too-corrupt-for-single-payer-health-care/

Klima CS. Unintended pregnancy. Consequences and solutions for a worldwide problem. J Nurse Midwifery 1998;43:483–91.

Kohler, Jillian Clare, and Guitelle Baghdadi-Sabeti. "The World Medicines Situation 2011." World Health Organization.[Links] (2011).

Kulier, R., et al. "Copper containing, framed intra-uterine devices for contraception (Review)."The Cochrane Library, Issue 4, 2008. Web accessed Dec 11th 2013 from: http://www.thecochranelibrary.com/userfiles/ccoch/file/Intrauterine%20devices/CD005347.pdf

Kumar, N., et al. Pharmaceutical Sales and Marketing: A rapidly evolving business. Tata Consultancy Services Limited. 2006-07.

Leonard, Donald. Bayer's new IUD draws debate on its benefits. Medill Reports . First published Feb 21, 2013. Accessed Dec 11 2013 from: http://news.medill.northwestern.edu/chicago/news.aspx?id=216409

Light, Donald W., and Joel Lexchin. "Foreign free riders and the high price of US medicines." BMJ: British Medical Journal 331.7522 (2005): 958.

Light, Donald W., and Rebecca Warburton. "Demythologizing the high costs of pharmaceutical research." BioSocieties 6.1 (2011): 34-50.

Light, Donald W., and Joel R. Lexchin. "Pharmaceutical research and development: what do we get for all that money?"

BMJ: British Medical Journal 345 (2012).

Lowes, Robert. Physicians Risk Lawsuits, Prison for Using Un-approved IUDs. Medscape.com. Published July 29, 2010. Accessed Dec 11 2013 from:
http://www.medscape.com/viewarticle/725988

Love, James, and Tim Hubbard. "Make drugs affordable: replace TRIPs-plus by R&D-plus." Bridges 8 (2004): 1-4.

Maurice, John. China to Upgrade its IUD Technology. Progress in Reproductive Health Research. Issue 60, 2002. Editor: Jitendra Khanna. Web accessed Dec 11, 2013.

MacIsaac, Laura, and Eve Espey. "Intrauterine contraception: the pendulum swings back." Obstetrics and gynecology clinics of North America 34.1 (2007): 91-111.

Martin, Roger L., and Sally Osberg. "Social entrepreneurship: the case for definition." Stanford social innovation review 5.2 (2007): 27-39.

Matheny, Gaverick. "Family planning programs: getting the most for the money." International Family Planning Perspectives 30.3 (2004): 134-138.

McArdle, Megan. US Consumers Foot the Bill for Cheap Drugs in Europe and Canada. Bloomberg View. Published October 14, 2013. Accessed March 3 2014 from:
http://www.bloomberg.com/news/2013-10-14/u-s-consumers-foot-the-bill-for-cheap-drugs-in-europe-and-canada.html

Miles, Donna. VA Outranks Private Sector in Health Care Patient Satisfaction. American Foreign Press Service. Published Jan 20, 2006. Accessed March 3, 2014 from:
http://www.defense.gov/news/newsarticle.aspx?id=14560

Milsom, Ian, et al. "Should profitability determine the availability of effective contraception?." The Lancet 355.9218 (2000): 1914-1915.

Moïse, P. and E. Docteur (2007), "Pharmaceutical Pricing and Reimbursement Policies in Mexico", OECD Health Working Paper No. 25, OECD, Paris.

Monea, Emily, and Adam Thomas. "Unintended pregnancy and taxpayer spending." Perspectives on Sexual and Reproductive Health 43.2 (2011): 88-93.

Moreland, Scott. "How Much Will It Cost to Achieve Egypt's Population Goals." POLICY Project (2000): 1-22.

Mosher, William D., and Charles F. Westoff. Trends in contraceptive practice, United States, 1965-76. US Department of Health and Human Services, Public Health Service, Office of Research, Statistics, and Technology, National Center for Health Statistics, 1982.

Mosher, William D., and William F. Pratt. "Contraceptive use in the United States, 1973–1988." Patient education and counseling 16.2 (1990): 163-172.

Mosher, William D., and Jo Jones. "Use of contraception in the United States: 1982-2008."Vital and health statistics. Series 23, Data from the National Survey of Family Growth 29 (2010): 1.

Mosher, William D., Jo Jones, and Joyce C. Abma. Intended and unintended births in the United States: 1982-2010. US Department of Health and Human Services, Centers for Disease Control and Prevention, National Center for Health Statistics, 2012.

Moskosky, S. B., et al. "Contraceptive methods available to patients of office-based physicians and Title X clinics—United States, 2009–2010." MMWR Morb Mortal Wkly Rep 60 (2011): 1-4.

Moynihan, Ray, & Mintzes, B. Sex, Lies, and Pharmaceuticals: How Drug Companies Plan to Profit from Female Sexual Dysfunction. Greystone Books, 2010.

National Family Planning & Reproductive Health Association. "Securing Affordable Contraceptive Drugs and Devices for Title X Providers". Policy Brief. Fall 2010.

Nelson, Anita L. "Safety, Efficacy, and Patient Acceptability of the Copper T-380A Intrauterine Contraceptive Device." Clinical Medicine Insights: Women's Health 2011.4 (2011): 35-50.

Neville, S., and Rankin, J. GlaxoSmithKline accused of paying rivals to delay generic medicine: OFT launches investigation into allegations GSK abused market dominance to keep price of antidepressant drug Seroxat high. The Guardian. Published April 19, 2013. Web accessed January 15, 2014 from:
http://www.theguardian.com/business/2013/apr/19/glaxosmithkline-gsk-oft-generic-seroxat-paroxetine

NICE. National Institute for Health and Clinical Excellence. Measuring effectiveness and cost effectiveness: the QALY. Accessed March 5th, 2014 from: http://www.nice.org.uk/newsroom/features/measuringeffectivenessandcosteffectivenesstheqaly.jsp

NICE. National Institute for Health and Clinical Excellence. Long-acting Reversible Contraception. 2005. Web accessed January 20 2014, available from:
http://www.nice.org.uk/nicemedia/live/10974/29909/29909.pdf

Nichols, et al. Are Market Forces Strong Enough To Deliver Efficient Health Care Systems? Confidence Is Waning. Health Affairs, 23, no.2 (2004):8-21

Noah, Yasmin. Bayardo Cruz, Buena Park Doctor, Has License Revoked After Using Non-FDA Approved IUDs on Patients. OC Weekly Blog. Published Jul7 17, 2012. Web accessed Dec 11,

2013 from: http://blogs.ocweekly.com/navelgazing/2012/07/bayardo_cruz.php

Norris, P., et al. "Drug promotion: what we know, what we have yet to learn (Reviews of materials in the WHO/HAI database on drug promotion). World Health Organization and Health Action International 2005

Okoye, Obianuju. The Future of Obamacare: Get Free Vacations: The Affordable Care Act and its impact on Medical Tourism [Kindle Edition]. Amazon Digital Services, Inc. Published February 8, 2014.

Ouellette, et al. v. Janet Miller et al. Civil No. 1:13-CV-00347-NT. Available from:
http://www.hpm.com/pdf/blog/Maine%20-%20PhRMA%20Import%20Law%20Complaint.pdf

Paltrow, Lynn M. How Indiana Is Making It Possible to Jail Women for Having Abortions. Political Research Associates. Published March 29, 2015. Web accessed April 11 2015 from: http://www.politicalresearch.org/2015/03/29/how-indiana-is-making-it-possible-to-jail-women-for-having-abortions//

Paris, V. and E. Docteur (2006), "Pharmaceutical Pricing and Reimbursement Policies in Canada", OECD Health Working Papers, No. 24, OECD Publishing. http://dx.doi.org/10.1787/346071162287

Paris, V. and E. Docteur (2008), "Pharmaceutical Pricing and Reimbursement Policies in Germany", OECD Health Working Papers, No. 39, OECD Publishing. http://dx.doi.org/10.1787/228483137521

PBS Frontline. So You Want to Buy Prescription Drugs in Canada? Published June 19 2003, accessed Dec 13 2013 from: http://www.pbs.org/wgbh/pages/frontline/shows/other/etc/so.html

PBS Newshour Report. Maine's prescription for drug savings: Go foreign. Aired December 31, 2013. Accessed January 10 2014 from: http://www.pbs.org/newshour/bb/health/july-dec13/drugs_12-31.html

Peipert, Jeffrey F., et al. "Continuation and satisfaction of reversible contraception." Obstetrics and gynecology 117.5 (2011): 1105.

Peipert, Jeffrey F., et al. "Preventing unintended pregnancies by providing no-cost contraception." Obstetrics & Gynecology 120.6 (2012): 1291-1297.

Perkes, Courtney. Doctor Accused of Medi-cal Fraud. Orange County Register. Published May 3rd, 2011. Accessed Dec 11, 2013 from: http://www.ocregister.com/articles/cal-298937-me-di-cruz.html

Pew Charitable Trusts. After Heparin: Protecting Consumers from the Risks of Substandard and Counterfeit Drugs. Washington, DC, March 2011; Accessed Feb 2014 from: http://www.pewtrusts.org/%20uploadedFiles/wwwpewtrustsorg/Reports/Health/Pew_Heparin_Final_HR.pdf

Pew Prescription Project. Fact sheet: Pharmaceutical Industry Marketing. January 28, 2009.

Politicofact.com. Michael Moore claims a majority favor a single-payer health care system. The Tampa Bay Times. Published Oct 1st 2009. Accessed March 12 2014 from: http://www.politifact.com/truth-o-meter/statements/2009/oct/01/michael-moore/michael-moore-claims-majority-favor-single-payer-h/

Postlethwaite D et al., A comparison of contraceptive procurement pre- and post-benefit change. Contraception. 2007. 76(5) 360–365.

Pritchett, Lant. "The cliff at the border." Equity and Growth in a Globalizing World (2006): 263.

Program for Appropriate Technology in Health (PATH). Intrauterine Devices Technology Opportunity Assessment: Prepared for the Merck for Mothers Program. 2013.

Ramirez, Francisco J., and Ann M. Starrs. "The Ending of IUD Sales in the United States: What Are the International Implications?." International Family Planning Perspectives 13.2 (1987): 71-74.

Reinhardt, Uwe E., Peter S. Hussey, and Gerard F. Anderson. "US health care spending in an international context." Health Affairs 23.3 (2004): 10-25.

Reinhardt, Uwe E. "The pricing of US hospital services: chaos behind a veil of secrecy." Health Affairs 25.1 (2006): 57-69.

Reinhardt, Uwe E. "The Disruptive Innovation of Price Transparency in Health Care. Viewpoint." JAMA 310.18 (2013): 1927-1928.

Rockerfeller, et al. Shining Light on the "Gray Market": An examination of why hospitals are forced to pay exorbitant prices for prescription drugs facing critical shortage. Committee on Oversight and Government Reform. (2012). Available from: http://democrats.oversight.house.gov/

Rode, Margaret. Obama Interview Shows Americans Highly Concerned About Drug Prices; Drug Importation Mentioned as Potential Solution. Pharmacy Checker Blog. Published February 4, 2011. Web accessed April 11, 2015 from: http://pharmacycheckerblog.com/obama-interview-shows-americans-highly-concerned-about-drug-prices-drug-importation-mentioned-as-potential-solution

Rode, Margaret. Drug Importation Bill Introduced by Senator Olympia Snowe. Pharmacy Checker Blog.Published February

18, 2011. Web accessed April 11, 2015 from: http://pharmacy-checkerblog.com/drug-importation-bill-introduced-by-senator-olympia-snowe

Rodriguez, Maria Isabel, et al. "Cost–benefit analysis of state-and hospital-funded postpartum intrauterine contraception at a university hospital for recent immigrants to the United States." Contraception 81.4 (2010): 304-308.

Rosenthal, Elizabeth. American Way of Birth, Costliest in the World. The New York Times. Published June 3 2013. Web accessed Dec 11 2013 from: http://www.nytimes.com/2013/07/01/health/americanway-of-birth-costliest-in-the-world.html?_r=0

Rovira, Juan. "Equity pricing as a strategy for improving the affordability of drugs in developing countries." Executive Summary. Workshop on Key Issues in Improving the Accessibility to drugs in Developing Countries. Washington DC. The World Bank. 20 June. Vol. 202. 2003.

Rumman, Ahmed. India Appeals Body Rejects Bayer's Plea on Nexavar. The Wall Street Journal. Published March 4, 2013.

Sack, Kevin and Connelly, Marjorie. In Poll, Wide Support for Government-Run Health. The New York Times. Published: June 20, 2009. Web accessed February 2, 2014 from: http://www.nytimes.com/2009/06/21/health/policy/21poll.html?_r=0

Safemedicines.org. Kentucky OBGYN Sentenced To Probation For Purchasing Counterfeit IUDs. Published Aug 12, 2013. Accessed Dec 11, 2013 from: http://www.safemedicines.org/2013/08/kentucky-obgyn-sentenced-to-probation-for-purchasing-counterfeit-iuds.html

Samuelson, Robert. Obama's Healthcare Headache. The Washington Post. Published Jan 12 2009 accessed Feb 28 2014 from: http://www.washingtonpost.com/wp-dyn/content/article/2009/01/11/AR2009011101895.html

Sarley, David, et al. "Options for contraceptive procurement: lessons learned from Latin America and the Caribbean." Habitat Debate 12.3 (2006): 10-11.

Secura GM, Allsworth JE, Madden T, et al. The Contraceptive CHOICE Project: reducing barriers to long-acting reversible contraception. Am J Obstet Gynecol 2010;203:115.e1-7.

Seelos, Christian, and Johanna Mair. "Entrepreneurs in service of the poor: models for business contributions to sustainable development." Business Horizons 48.3 (2005): 241-246.

Serbanescu F, Stupp P and Westoff CF, Contraception matters: two approaches to analyzing evidence of the abortion decline in Georgia, International Perspectives on Sexual and Reproductive Health, 2010, 36(2):99–110.

Sifferlin, Alexandra. Breaking Down GlaxoSmithKline's Billion-Dollar Wrongdoing: What the drug company did to promote Paxil, Wellbutrin and Avandia illegally — and what it meant for patients. Time Health & Family. Published July 05, 2012. Web accessed January 15, 2014, from: http://healthland.time.com/2012/07/05/breaking-down-glaxosmithklines-billion-dollar-wrongdoing/#ixzz2raTBmyCZ

Silverman, Ed. What The Supreme Court Ruling Means For Pharma. Forbes. Published June 28, 2012. Web accessed January 20 2013 from: http://www.forbes.com/sites/edsilverman/2012/06/28/what-the-supreme-court-ruling-means-for-pharma/

Silverman, Ed. Will Americans Be Allowed To Import Prescription Drugs? Forbes. Published Dec 31 2013, web accessed January 28 2014 from: http://www.forbes.com/sites/edsilverman/2013/12/31/will-americans-be-allowed-to-import-prescription-drugs/

Sivin, Irving. "Utility and drawbacks of continuous use of a copper T IUD for 20 years." Contraception 75.6 (2007): S70-S75.

Smith, Richard. "Medical journals are an extension of the marketing arm of pharmaceutical companies." PLoS Medicine 2.5 (2005): e138.

Sonfield, Adam. "Popularity disparity: attitudes about the IUD in Europe and the United States." Guttmacher Policy Review 10.4 (2007): 19-24.

Sonfield, Adam. "Abortion clinics and contraceptive services: opportunities and challenges." Guttmacher Policy Review 14.2 (2011a).

Sonfield, Adam, et al. "The public costs of births resulting from unintended pregnancies: national and state-level estimates." Perspectives on Sexual and Reproductive Health 43.2 (2011b): 94-102.

Spurling, Geoffrey K., et al. "Information from pharmaceutical companies and the quality, quantity, and cost of physicians' prescribing: a systematic review." PLoS medicine 7.10 (2010): e1000352.

Stanback, John. "Perspectives on Local Manufacture of Contraceptives in Developing Countries." (1997).

St. James, Janet. Grapevine doctor defends using bargain IUDs. WFAA. Published Oct 21, 2010. Accessed Dec 11, 2013 from: http://www.wfaa.com/news/health/Grapevine-doctor-defends-using-bargain-IUDs-105496683.html

Stubbs, Esther, and Adrianna Schamp. "The evidence is in. Why are IUDs still out? Family physicians' perceptions of risk and indications." Canadian Family Physician 54.4 (2008): 560-566.

Suisse, Credit. "Global Wealth Report 2013." Zurich: Crédit Suisse. https://publications.credit-suisse.com/tasks/render/file(2013).

Takeshita, Chikako. Negotiating Acceptability of the IUD. Diss. Virginia Polytechnic Institute and State University, 2004.

Texas v. Women's Integrated Healthcare P.A. et al. Web accessed Dec 11, 2013 from: https://www.oag.state.tx.us/newspubs/releases/2010/102110womens_healthcare_pop.pdf

Thailand Government. Thailand Medical Tourism [Kindle Edition]. Amazon Digital Services, Inc. Published September 16, 2011.

THE PEOPLE, v. EDUARDO JOSE GUZMAN. Court of Appeal, Second District, California. 12 Dec. 2011. Web accessed January 28, 2014 from: http://caselaw.findlaw.com/ca-court-of-appeal/1588113.html

Thiery, M. "Pioneers of the intrauterine device." European J. of Contraception and Reproductive Healthcare 2.1 (1997): 15-23.

Thomas, Adam. Policy Solutions for Preventing Unplanned Pregnancy. Center on Children and Families at Brookings Institution. 2012.

Thomas, Katie, and Schmidt, Michael. Glaxo Agrees to Pay $3 Billion in Fraud Settlement. International New York Times. Published July 2, 2012. Web accessed Janaury 15th, 2014 from: http://www.nytimes.com/2012/07/03/business/glaxosmithkline-agrees-to-pay-3-billion-in-fraud-settlement.html?_r=0

Thompson, Kirsten MJ, Diana Greene Foster, and Cynthia C. Harper. "Increased Use of Intrauterine Contraception in California, 1997 to 2007." Women's Health Issues 21.6 (2011): 425-430.

Todd, Maria. Employer's Guide to Medical Tourism Benefit Design. Productivity Press. Published September 15, 2014.

Trussell, James, et al. "The economic value of contraception: a comparison of 15 methods." American journal of public health 85.4 (1995): 494-503.

Trussell, James, et al. "Preventing unintended pregnancy: the cost-effectiveness of three methods of emergency contraception." American Journal of Public Health 87.6 (1997a): 932-937.

Trussell, James, et al. "Medical care cost savings from adolescent contraceptive use." Family Planning Perspectives (1997b): 248-295.

Trussell, James, et al. "Cost effectiveness of contraceptives in the United States." Contraception 79.1 (2009): 5-14.

Trussell, James. "Update on the cost-effectiveness of contraceptives in the United States." Contraception 82. (2010)

Trussell, James. "Update on and correction to the cost-effectiveness of contraceptives in the United States." Contraception 85.6 (2012a): 611.

Trussell, James, et al. "Burden of unintended pregnancy in the United States: potential savings with increased use of long-acting reversible contraception." Contraception(2012b).

Ungar, Rick. The Bomb Buried In Obamacare Explodes Today-Hallelujah! Forbes.Published December 2nd, 2011. Web accessed January 28th 2014 from: http://www.forbes.com/sites/rickungar/2011/12/02/the-bomb-buried-in-obamacare-explodes-today-halleluja/

United Nations. Department of Economic and Social Affairs. Population Division. World contraceptive use 2005. 2006; United Nations publication.

United Nations. Department of Economic and Social Affairs.

Population Division. World contraceptive use 2009. 2009; United Nations publication. Accessed Jan 12 2013 from: http:// www.un.org/esa/population/publications/contraceptive2009/ contraceptive2009.htm

United States Department of Commerce. Pharmaceutical price controls in OECD countries: implications for US consumers, pricing, research and development and innovation. Washington, DC: USDC, 2004.

US Attorney's Office Western District of Kentucky. Owner Of Bluegrass Women's Healthcare In Elizabethtown Charged With Health Care Fraud, Mail Fraud, Misbranding And Smuggling Published March 21 2013, web accessed Dec 11 2013 from: http://www.justice.gov/usao/kyw/news/2013/20130321-01.html

US Attorney's Office Western District of Kentucky. Owner Of Bluegrass Women's Healthcare In Elizabethtown Ordered To Pay Victims $50,663.31 For Misbranding. Published Dec 13 2013, web accessed Dec 20 2013 from: http://www.justice.gov/ usao/kyw/news/2013/20131213-01.html

US Department of Justice Press Release. September 30, 2011: Pine Bluff Doctor Sentenced in Health Care Fraud and Mis-branding Case. Web accessed Dec 11 2013 from: http:// www.fda.gov/ICECI/CriminalInvestigations/ucm274435.htm

US General Accounting Office. Canadian Health Insurance: lessons for the United States. Washington, DC: General Accounting Office, 1991. (GAO/HRD-91-90).

US Senate, Joint Economic Committee. The benefits of med-ical research and the role of the NIH. Washington (DC): The Committee. 2000 May 17.

Ventura, Stephanie J., et al. "Estimated pregnancy rates and rates of pregnancy outcomes for the United States, 1990-2008." National vital statistics reports: from the Centers for Disease Control and

Prevention, National Center for Health Statistics, National Vital Statistics System 60.7 (2012): 1.

Wei, Marlynn. "Should prizes replace patents? A critique of the Medical Innovation Prize Act of 2005." Boston University Journal of Science & Technology Law (2007).

Weisbrod, Burton A., and Craig L. LaMay. "Mixed signals: public policy and the future of health care R&D." Health Affairs 18.2 (1999): 112-125.

Wen, Jin, et al. "Comparative cost?effectiveness of three intrauterine devices: a multi?center randomized trial." Journal of Evidence?Based Medicine 3.2 (2010): 76-82.

Westoff. Recent trends in abortion and contraception in 12 countries, DHS Analytical Studies, Calverton, Maryland: ORC Macro, 2005, No. 8.

Wight, Patty. Federal Judge Deals Blow to Maine Law Allowing Prescription Drug Imports. Maine Public Broadcasting. Published February 24, 2015. Web accessed April 11 2015 from: http://news.mpbn.net/post/federal-judge-deals-blow-maine-law-allowing-prescription-drug-imports

Winner, Brooke, et al. "Effectiveness of long-acting reversible contraception." New England Journal of Medicine 366.21 (2012): 1998-2007.

World Health Organization. "The TCu380A Intrauterine Contraceptive Device (IUD). Specification, prequalification and guidelines for procurement, 2010."

Ziegler, Michael G., Pauline Lew, and Brian C. Singer. "The accuracy of drug information from pharmaceutical sales representatives." Jama 273.16 (1995): 1296-1298.

Zimmerman, Eric. "Steele denounces healthcare as 'socialist utopia'" Thehill.com. Published March 18, 2010, Available from: http://thehill.com/blogs/blog-briefing-room/news/87753-steele-denounces-healthcare-as-socialist-utopia

www.ingramcontent.com/pod-product-compliance
Lightning Source LLC
Chambersburg PA
CBHW060620290526
45793CB00001B/92